JAPANESE GARDENS
IN A WEEKEND®

JAPANESE GARDENS IN A WEEKEND®

Robert Ketchell

hamlyn

First published in Great Britain in 2001
by Hamlyn, a division of
Octopus Publishing Group Ltd
2–4 Heron Quays, London E14 4JP

This edition published in 2005

Distributed in the United States and Canada by
Sterling Publishing Co., Inc.
387 Park Avenue South, New York, NY 10016–8810

'In a Weekend' is the registered property of Sterling
Publishing Co., Inc., 387 Park Avenue South, New York, NY
10016, and is used by permission.

ISBN–13: 978-0-60061428-9
ISBN–10: 0-600-61428-X

A CIP catalogue record for this book is available from the
British Library

Printed and bound in China

10 9 8 7 6 5 4 3

CONTENTS

INTRODUCTION

Japanese gardens have a particular allure all of their own. They appear so still, yet can dance before our eyes, and fill us with a profound sense of beauty. Spending some time lost in reverie in one of the Kyoto temple gardens, sitting on a wooden veranda in front of a garden created hundreds of years ago, is one of life's great experiences.

One of the extraordinary aspects of looking at Japanese gardens today is that we can feel a common bond with garden creators of 1,000 years ago. What they strove after then is just as valid now, as we attempt to create beauty within our own gardens. The Japanese garden tradition can become a well of inspiration to be dipped into, each time coming up with an insight that may eventually change the way we look at and understand our own gardens. To study the Japanese garden tradition is also to open our eyes to new ways of seeing gardens and the

Below The Japanese garden is often seen from a path. The pathway allows the viewer to engage with the garden scenery.

landscape – we can look again at the familiar, and find fresh ways of expressing ourselves.

Early Japanese gardens

The tradition of creating gardens in Japan goes back a very long way. The earliest historical reference to a garden dates back to AD 74, and describes the Emperor of the time looking into his *koi* pond and admiring his fish. Quite possibly, the original idea of having a garden in the grounds of the Emperor's dwelling came from contacts with China. From a variety of literary sources, we can put together a simple picture of what these earliest gardens looked like. They were centred around a pond, and some of the ponds were clearly large enough to launch a boat on. Winding streams abounded. The planting was varied and rich, each season being marked by ceremony and flowers.

Japan is blessed with a wonderfully rich flora. The islands that make up Japan vary widely in both climate and topography, allowing for an abundant range of native plants to thrive. In early Japanese society, every seasonal change was marked by ceremony and celebrations: the Iris Festival and the Red Leaf Festival are two examples. The gardens also acted as locations for the ceremonies to be enacted.

The earliest gardens in Japan were endeavours to recreate nature in a refined manner, representing a spirit-blessed world. The native religion in Japan, Shinto, was a religion born of the landscape. The gods and ceremonials of Shinto are deeply connected

with the seasons and the landscape. Certain parts of the landscape are held to be sacred, and at such sites people can directly approach the gods themselves. Whole mountains (for example Mount Fuji), mountaintops, springs, caves, waterfalls, groves of trees and even individual trees may all be the homes of gods.

In AD 552, Buddhism reached Japan from Korea, and this heralded a resurgence in cultural development. With it came a means of writing and new ideas on the organization of the Imperial court. Around AD 793, the Emperor decided to settle the capital on the gently sloping south-facing land between two rivers. Protected to the north by mountains, it was deemed by *feng shui* to be a fitting place. With the establishment of the city of Kyoto, the garden culture flourished and was to become an essential part of the lives of the Imperial classes. This time is known as the Heian period, and it saw the emergence of a distinctive garden style.

The Heian period (AD 794–1185)

Many of the Heian gardens were estates that ranged over many acres; deer were hunted in some of the larger gardens. Large ponds were almost invariably to be found at the centre of the gardens, which would also make extensive use of the abundant supply of natural water. Boating was a very popular activity, and there are several references to boating trips in the Heian period novel *The Tale of Genji*, by Murasaki Shikibu (translated by Edward Seidensticker, Secker &

Warburg, 1976): 'On the day of the excursion the emperor was attended by his whole court, the princes and the rest ... Music came from boats rowed out over the lake, and there was an infinite variety of Chinese and Korean dancing. Reed and drum echoed through the grounds.'

The Heian period has a rich literary tradition; poetry was used by the educated classes, and many poems derive their imagery from the gardens. The gardens must have been wonderful places, filled with movement, colour and sound. There were also quieter, smaller gardens attached to the

dwellings in courtyard areas between the buildings. These gardens developed in the open spaces which were required in order to allow light into the buildings. The gardens could be enjoyed simply by sliding back panels to allow in light and air. Spring-flowering plants were particularly prized, but a whole range of plants was employed in these spaces. Chrysanthemums were widely planted for autumn colour. Azaleas were collected in the mountains, and hybridizing soon resulted in many garden varieties.

The gardens were designed by aristocrats themselves, since gardening

was accepted to be an activity of the educated and refined. In the late 11th century, a manual of landscape gardening known as the *Sakuteiki* was published. It represents an attempt to summarize all the known and accepted techniques for siting and creating a garden. It provides us with a vivid picture of the art of gardening at the time, and also testifies to the importance that gardens were held in. One of the first pieces of advice given is to use the natural landscape as your model. Copy from nature. If you are creating a waterfall in your garden, go into the landscape and see what a

Above The 'Silver Pavilion', Ginkaku-ji, Kyoto, was originally created to enjoy moon-viewing, a popular pastime in the 14th century.

waterfall looks like, how it is caused. Then come back to your garden and recreate what you understood and saw. The reader is also encouraged to study the works of past masters, indicating that there was already a body of knowledge that was seen as representing a tradition. The *Sakuteiki* is still studied by garden creators today.

Part of the Buddhist doctrine which inspired garden creators dealt with the idea of change, and the view that the world we see is only one aspect of reality. This encouraged the garden creators to view the garden space as a landscape map, depicting an idealized version of Paradise. A single rock in a pond could be seen simply as a stone, or as a mountain rising

from the sea. The garden could begin to draw upon a wide source of imagery to present to the viewer. Famous beauty spots were recreated in the garden scenery, and even famed trees would be alluded to in the planting. One aristocrat had salt water carried to Kyoto – a distance overland of over 110km (70 miles) – so that he could have vats of salt water boiled on the shore of his pond as a means of reminding him of childhood landscape memories. Temple complexes were rendered after mandalas, the traditional Buddhist geometric depictions of Paradise. The garden was a place of transformation wherein everyday reality could be transformed and transcended – a place of imagination.

Zen influences

The end of the Heian period saw power shifting decisively away from the aristocracy in favour of the military classes. With the rise of the feudal clan chiefs, wealth spread beyond the Imperial compounds, and gardens gradually ceased to be the preserve of the few. The military favoured the Zen form of Buddhism, which became one of the profoundest influences on Japanese culture. It was at a Zen temple that the *karesansui* or 'dry landscape style' of garden was to reach its zenith with the creation of the famous gravel and rock garden of Ryoan-ji. Created in 1499, this garden still exerts a powerful pull and attracts thousands of visitors every year; and has been designated a World Heritage Site. The garden takes the idea of suggestion to an extreme, where the rock placements have been variously interpreted as a depiction of the spring-appearing Pleiades star cluster, Paradise Isles of legend, mountain peaks appearing above mists, or a tigress leading her cubs across a river. The stones themselves remain coyly mute and hold their own counsel.

The gardens had developed into a fusion of ideas derived from religion, myth, the natural landscape and Chinese landscape painting. Clearly, the garden can both be seen in its physical form and enjoyed for its symbolic contents. Gardens were created to feast the eye as much as the mind and other senses. The garden retained a sense of remaining close to the source of all things, which was appreciated as being nature.

The Tea Ceremony
The garden tradition spread and popularized even further in the 16th century with the rise of the Tea Ceremony, which involved the ritual preparation and serving of tea between host and guests. This ceremony was performed in a special Tea Room or House, and the guest passed through a garden to reach the Tea Room. The Tea House was modelled after a rustic dwelling, and the garden represents a path leading through a mountain landscape. The use of stepping stones became widespread in all kinds of gardens after their adoption and use in the Tea Garden. The practice of using stone lanterns and water basins is also derived from the Tea Garden. Planting in the Tea Gardens was deliberately restrained and naturalistic, so as not to disturb the visitor; showy flowering plants were avoided in favour of evergreens, maples, ferns and mosses. In the Tea Room itself, a flower arrangement reflecting the season is displayed in the position of greatest honour.

Today, gardens in Japan are highly seasonal in their display of colour. During spring there is a succession of dazzling displays of plum and cherry trees, irises and azaleas, and autumn is marked by the brilliant leaf colour of Japanese maple trees. In between, the gardens have little in the way of colour displays, remaining a subtle blend of thousands of shades of green, more dependent on shape and form than colour, to give meaning and purpose to the space.

Modern Japanese gardens
The pattern of Japanese gardens has been created, developed and passed on from one generation to the next. Today, in Japan, the next generation of gardeners is acquiring the skills to maintain ancient gardens, as well as to create new ones. The finest traditional style has always been the preserve of those with the means to afford to build and maintain highly complex gardens, but the underlying ideas that make up the fabric of that tradition are accessible to anyone who cares to look. These ideas can enrich your own view of gardens and the landscape by heightening your understanding of both. Many of the ideas expressed through the projects in this book can be applied for use in garden projects that are not solely influenced by Japanese style. Looking at the way in which another culture creates its gardens can provide a great deal of inspiration for our own.

Left The preparation and serving of tea in the Tea Ceremony is inspired by the arts, philosophy and religion.

Careful planning before beginning work on the garden will lead to a more satisfying and accomplished end result. Planning begins with a thorough understanding of the site and what you are hoping to create within it.

PLANNING

Planning

MAKING A SKETCH PLAN

Before you start any construction, however simple the project might be, you should draw up a detailed overhead sketch plan of the intended finished feature or garden area. A little time and trouble taken at the beginning on such a plan, following the steps outlined below, will reap many rewards later in the construction process.

Right Careful planning allows you to visualize the garden before it is actually completed.

Some of the projects in this book are self-contained, so all you need to decide is where in the garden to position the chosen feature. With other projects, you have more freedom to create your own design within the overall concept of the project. In these cases, you should bear in mind the key design concepts listed on pages 16–19.

At the planning stage, it can be helpful to take a few photographs, and also to draw out some rough three-dimensional sketches, showing very loosely the shapes you have in mind. This will help you to imagine better how the finished article will look. Remember that you may be taking up to three weekends to complete a project, so it will be very difficult to keep everything in your head. Above all, with any plan design, be flexible in your ideas and use the plan to understand the way things will look on the ground. When you start work on site you will be making decisions and alterations in the face of practicalities, but if you have immersed yourself in the making of a plan you should have a clear idea of where you are heading.

1   Sketch out a survey of the site as it exists, trying to take in as much information as possible regarding orientation, existing planting and features, contours and changes in level. Make note of other information, such as types of boundary (hedge or fencing), views out beyond the garden area or poorly drained patches. Taking photographs will help you memorize the site when sitting

Left When choosing the planting pay attention to the blend of textures as well as colours.

down to plan the garden, although looking and sketching will always be of more value, as you will be seeing what is really there.

2   Take measurements on site; this will allow you to draw a scale plan on paper. The more measurements you take the better, since you will then be able to cross-check. Take at least two measurements to each significant point.

3   Draw out the whole site to scale on the plan. Establish where the main

viewing points are and divide the area roughly into three parts from each location. This will establish the foreground, middle ground and background for the principal views.

4   Consider any changes in existing levels and mark these on the plan. Plan to reuse any good topsoil on the site. Likewise, plan to install land drains in the area if water retention is a problem. Remember that altering the existing contours of a garden can create drainage problems as well as solve them.

5   If you are planning a water feature, decide on the best position for this and design the remainder of the garden space around it. Think how deep the pond will need to be, especially if you wish to include some fish (see page 34).

6   Mark on the plan the main routes across the site. Look at the possibility of integrating the lines of movement across the garden with the potential location of focal points. Remember to give some reason or purpose to alterations in

Right Water features should always be carefully sited so as to give maximum visual and aural effect.

stepping-stone path encourages the viewer to look downward at where his or her feet are landing. Combining the nature of the path with planting as a screen, it is possible for the viewer 'suddenly' to come across a particular scene or view. Where you use a stepping-stone path, place a wide, flat stone as a landing at a point where you want the viewer to repose and take in the garden.

9 Plan the detail of the ground cover, planting, lawn, gravel and other surfaces. Be practical and realistic about what you can achieve and can afford to achieve. Lawns and grass areas can provide attractive contrasts to gravel areas, though you will need to consider how to separate the gravel and grass. Large areas of planting can be difficult to maintain without some commitment of time. Consider as you plan how the garden is going to be looked after. When you become familiar with your plan, you can use it to move around the 'garden', imagining how every corner will look and feel.

10 Plan the detail of the siting and distribution of the planting. If the earth and stone arrangements make up the skeleton of the garden, then the flesh on the bones is the planting. The planting softens and subtly draws together the various parts of the design. Think about the height and spread of plants, as there will be an ideal proportion to the garden. You will need to be prepared to prune plants to maintain an optimum height and spread. You may have to grow on some of the planting to reach eventually the height and shape you see in your mind's eye. Your detailed sketch plan should now be complete, and you are ready to make it into reality.

the directions of paths; do not introduce a change of direction for no obvious reason.

7 Locate the main focal points on the plan; this includes waterfalls, streams, rocks, stone lanterns, water basins, individual plant specimens and so on. The focal points should be sited in conjunction with the lines of sight from the principal viewing areas. Remember to plan the views so that they have the three stages represented, as discussed above. You may find that you cannot easily fit everything in; in that case, consider using fewer elements,

or try moving the relative position of the features. Use your developing plan drawing to work through the practical problems of implementation. As you put features into the scheme, think about how they will be built, and what will be involved in order to create them.

8 Consider in detail the nature of the surfaces of the paths leading into and through the garden. The types of path will influence the way the viewer will see the garden. Smooth, wide, flat paths allow the viewer to walk with head up, taking in the scenery. Conversely, a

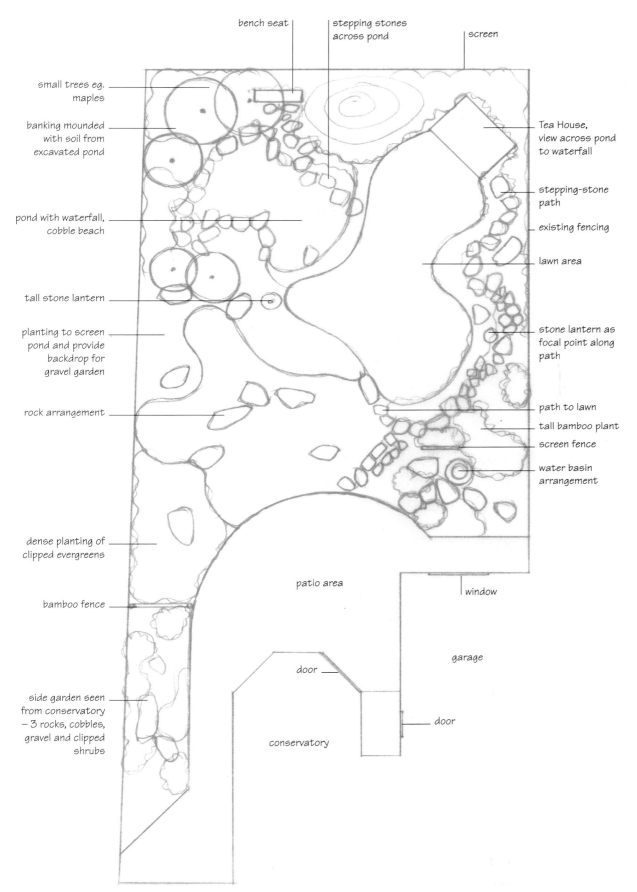

bench seat

stepping stones across pond

screen

small trees eg. maples

banking mounded with soil from excavated pond

pond with waterfall, cobble beach

tall stone lantern

planting to screen pond and provide backdrop for gravel garden

rock arrangement

dense planting of clipped evergreens

bamboo fence

side garden seen from conservatory – 3 rocks, cobbles, gravel and clipped shrubs

Tea House, view across pond to waterfall

stepping-stone path

existing fencing

lawn area

stone lantern as focal point along path

path to lawn

tall bamboo plant

screen fence

water basin arrangement

patio area

window

garage

door

door

conservatory

Left A sketch plan should show all the existing structures and features that you intend to keep as well as the proposed new elements.

KEY DESIGN CONCEPTS

There is no magic formula for creating Japanese gardens, but there are certain key elements that can be helpful if you are confident enough to tackle your own design rather than following the set projects included in this book. Learning to design a garden involves training your eye and imagination to work together.

Rather than there being a ready-made set of rules, there are several ideas that draw the attention of the designer to an awareness of the possibilities of the site, and to the individual qualities of the materials he or she is working with. These ideas are presented below as a series of guidelines and sources of inspiration for the designer.

Three basic zones

A garden, like a painting, is always composed of three distinct parts: the foreground, the middle ground, and the background. This immediately gives you a way of ordering the site into manageable zones of activity, guiding you to the places to locate features within the composition. The garden essentially becomes a series of views unfolding before the viewer as they approach the garden or move around it. Therefore, one of your first tasks is to consider how the garden is to be approached and seen. The approach to the garden prepares the viewer for what is ahead. Screening the garden and not revealing too much is desirable, as this will heighten the sense of expectation.

Structure and framework

Although Japanese gardens often appear to be put together in a very naturalistic, unstructured way, there is always a very carefully considered 'framework' that underlies them. The garden is composed of a series of 'masses' (plants, rocks and so on) organized on a series of levels (contours, slopes and so on). Therefore the first form of the garden is its underlying

Right A garden scene is built up of a series of 'layers'.

Left Triangular relationships between garden elements are a key design concept.

ground shapes, which will need to be organized to suit where you need elevation and depressions. The placement of the stones among the ground shapes defines still further the overall structure (ideas governing the exact placement of stones are discussed below, and on page 26).

Triangular relationships

The garden design can be seen as a series of invisible lines snaking out and touching each element of the composition. The relationships that are created between the rocks and plant shapes are based on asymmetrical triangles. This asymmetric arrangement of relationships creates a sense of movement and energy. The vertical lines of a composition will suggest the relative position of forms and imply depth. Horizontal planes establish a feeling of stability and breadth. Transitions and connections in perspective relationships are established by diagonal lines linking the vertical and horizontal planes.

Space and rhythm

Line and mass are defined and balanced by establishing areas of 'empty space' (*yohaku* in Japanese). It is very important in creating gardens not to fill every inch of the canvas, but to allow room for simple open spaces that exist to act as a contrast to the more active areas of the design. Open spaces can be created by the flat reflective surface of water, lawn areas, or areas beneath overhanging foliage. The garden composition needs to establish a rhythm of opening and closing as the eye of the viewer scans across it, or as the viewer walks around the garden. This is a rhythm that the viewer will be naturally attuned to and rested by.

Texture and energy

The garden composition uses the quality of duality in nature deliberately to create a multiplicity of textures – open/closed, smooth/rough, light/dark, large leaves/fine leaves. Through the interplay of these qualities, energy will be generated within the composition; the generation of 'energy' is one of the fundamental requisites of the garden. Textures can be played off one against another. By placing fine-leaved plants in the background of a composition and large-leaved specimens in

the foreground, you can imply that the space recedes further than it actually does. The opposite reaction can be achieved by reversing the process. It is the small that makes the large look larger, the bright that makes the dark look darker, and the incomplete that allows us to imagine the complete.

Stones with very rugged or fissured surfaces are best placed in the foreground as their texture draws the eye towards them. Smooth rounded stones will appear to recede into the background when placed with rough stones. A watercourse created with smooth rounded stones will appear to move more slowly than a stream created with rough, angular boulders. Placing a smaller flat stone at the base of a tall, vertical stone will enhance the stature of the taller stone. This deliberate contrast of forms and textures can also create a sense of the movement of energy. The Japanese garden expresses a paradox: while the balance of its design and composition appear very tranquil and placid, much is made of the use of energy in the design. To the Japanese and Chinese gardeners and artists, this was understood to be the working of yin and yang forces, the interdependent movement of which generates all life.

Colour

The preference in Oriental art is for monochrome, because it is felt that the greatest degree of suggestion can be gained in this way and the imagination of the viewer more fully engaged. Masses of colour can overwhelm the eye, whereas a single flower will hold the attention of the viewer completely.

Suggestion

It is rarely successful to overfill the scenery of the garden – it usually results in overcrowding the garden landscape and confusing the original intention. Suggestion can be used to good effect. For example, when creating a stepping-stone path, you could

Above
Compositions are created by arranging objects in asymmetric triangles.

Right Stepping stones through gravel can inject a view with energy.

add a side path that appears to lead off in another direction. The fact that the path actually leads nowhere will imply that the space is larger than it really is. Similarly, running gravel areas right up to fences and boundaries allows the viewer to imagine the garden extending beyond its physical boundaries.

Asymmetry

Irregularity is more interesting to the eye than regular or formal, visually predictable shapes. This is evident in the use of asymmetrical relationships when arranging stones and plants. It can also be seen in other important features such as the detailing of a streamcourse or pond bank.

Simplicity

Simplicity rather than elaboration is more likely to lay bare the soul of what is being presented. Elaborate decoration draws attention to itself; thus the viewer's attention remains on the surface. A composition is complete when

not one further element may be added, nor taken away, without destroying the sense of harmony and unity. In creating the work on the ground you are constantly asking the question: 'Does this really need to be there?' This prevents you getting carried away in the thrill of all the activity.

Impermanence

Perishability is seen as an essential quality of the garden. Bamboo is used extensively in Japanese gardens for fencing and other purposes. It is accepted that part of the natural cycle

of the garden is that the bamboo will need to be replaced every few years. Relative perishability is contrasted against the seemingly never-changing rocks that resist everything nature hurls at them. The cherry blossom is particularly revered in Japan because it is so short-lived at the peak of its beauty, as is the camellia flower.

Scale and perspective

Scale may be regarded as being a flexible concept in the hands of the garden designer or artist. False perspective can also be employed in composition.

For example, the placement of tall elements in the foreground and similar, smaller elements in the background will increase the sense of depth. Bold detail in the foreground will appear to bring the forms closer to the eye, while blurred detail and softer outlines will appear to recede into the distance.

Space

In a Japanese garden, space is usually implied, and not defined by enclosure. Enclosure is nearly always used, but in such a way as to create a separation of the garden space from the 'everyday world'. In small spaces, the size of elements is not necessarily scaled down to suit the size of the area. The implied space is intended to take the viewer beyond any physical boundaries that may be present.

Using symbols

Symbolism is one way through which the viewer may enter the landscape beyond the purely material level. The Japanese garden follows the universal pattern of the garden as an expression of the Paradise model; in Christian mythology this is the Garden of Eden. It also represents the transition between the worlds of the sacred and the profane. The garden has developed to take on the role of the temple precinct, and it is the place where we seek (or have the potential to seek) space beyond the everyday world. The symbolism involved in any particular culture is an expression of the spiritual language of that culture. The Japanese garden tradition inevitably has been heavily influenced by Taoist, Buddhist and Shinto symbolism and iconography: Mount Horai (*Shumisen*), Crane and Tortoise islands, the use of water as purifying agent, mountains and clouds, pine trees and so on.

Guiding the viewer

The intention in designing the garden is to present the viewer with enough visual clues that suggest an implied order to the composition to stimulate his or her imagination. The role of the viewer is crucial to this kind of garden. The garden may be said to remain incomplete until the viewer is present in the garden space. The garden then becomes complete through the interaction of the imagination of the viewer with the garden design.

The attention of the viewer can be subtly guided around the scenery, being led from one focal point to the next. This will also establish a rhythm and sense of order in the composition. In this way, the composition is gradually unfolded to the viewer just like a scroll painting. This works as well for gardens that are intended to be seen from certain fixed viewing positions, as it does within the larger stroll-through type of garden. Gardens seen from fixed positions are often much wider than they are deep, and they cannot be visually taken in without the viewer turning his or her head to one side or the other.

Left There will be an ideal balance in the relative height and density of groups of planting.

The most appropriate materials for your Japanese-style garden will generally be natural rather than man-made. However, although these materials are most suited to and work best in these types of garden they may need replacing more often.

MATERIALS

CONCRETE AND MORTAR

Concrete is used in several key operations in the projects in this book: laying foundations for water features, fixing the bases of fence posts, bedding cobbles and stepping stones, setting bridges and so on. Mortar is used in brick walls and copings, edging paths and lining streams. They are both relatively easy to make and use, and should not deter you when deciding on which project to undertake.

Making concrete

To make a quantity of concrete, you will need to mix cement, sharp sand and aggregate – this consists of stones of about 2cm (¾in) in diameter – in the following proportions: 1 part cement, 1½ parts sand and 2½ parts aggregate. You can mix these in small quantities on a board or in a barrow with a spade. Then make a hollow in the mix, and fill it almost to the top with water. Gradually mix the two together until you have a firm mix. For large quantities, it may be advisable to hire a concrete mixer.

You can also get ready-mixed concrete from a supplier, but remember that the area to be concreted must be thoroughly prepared before it is delivered, and that the supplier will need easy access to the site. You will also need to spread and level the concrete very quickly before it starts to set; a team of helpers is essential.

Laying concrete foundations

Mark out the area with pegs and string, and dig out the soil to a depth of about 20cm (8in). Drive in pegs all around the perimeter, so that their flat tops are level with the desired finished level of concrete. Check they are all level by laying a long piece of wood on top of them and using a spirit level. Remove the string, and nail wooden planks, laid on their sides, to the inside of the levelling pegs. Add a 10cm (4in) layer of hardcore, spread it level, and compact it firmly. Pour in the concrete mix and spread it into the edges and corners with a spade to a depth slightly higher than the planks. Slide a wooden plank

LAYING CONCRETE FOUNDATIONS

concrete

wooden beam to remove excess concrete and to level the surface

10cm (4in) layer of hardcore

wooden planks

wooden pegs

or beam across the top of the planks to remove the excess and level the surface. Then smooth the surface. Protect the concrete with plastic sheeting for about ten days, until it has set firm.

Setting fence posts

Dig a hole 60cm (2ft) deep, and about 25cm (10in) in diameter, for each post. Place the post in the hole and backfill with concrete. As you are doing this, push several pieces of broken brick or stone into the mix. This will give it additional weight and strength. Make sure the post is upright by checking it with a spirit level or plumb line. Make two checks, at right angles to one another, to ensure the post is absolutely upright. When setting out a number of posts in a line, put the two end posts in position first, and lightly 'tension' a string between them. This will give you the correct line for the remainder of the posts. You can also check this by eye, by looking along the line of posts to see if they are positioned neatly one behind another.

SETTING FENCE POSTS

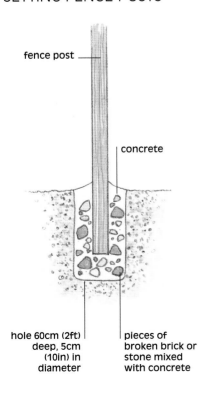

fence post

concrete

hole 60cm (2ft) deep, 5cm (10in) in diameter

pieces of broken brick or stone mixed with concrete

Above Wooden posts for fencing can be charred as a means of preservation.

Opposite Concrete can be laid over waterproof liners to create a pond base.

Using mortar

To make mortar, mix 1 part cement with 4 parts sharp sand. Add water carefully, and mix thoroughly to obtain a firm yet malleable consistency. In freezing weather, add a few drops (no more) of washing-up liquid. Mortar can also be waterproofed by adding a proprietary additive in the quantities indicated by the manufacturer. For brick walls and copings, use a pointing trowel to apply a bed of mortar 2cm (¾in) deep, and bed the bricks into the mortar by tapping them down with the edge of the trowel. Check that they are level in both directions with a spirit level. Remove the excess with the trowel as the mortar begins to firm, but before it sets.

Mortar can also be used to waterproof a streamcourse. Lay a bed of mortar 5cm (2in) deep over the liner on the bed of the streamcourse. Smooth the surface, taking care to work the mortar into any gaps between the stones lining the sides of the stream. While the mortar is still soft, you can press cobbles or pebbles into the mortar bed; alternatively, lay a thin covering of gravel over the damp mortar, and then gently tamp it down into the mortar.

STONE

In the context of the Japanese garden, a stone or rock arrangement is one of the most important design elements. This has been so since the earliest gardens were created in Japan, and garden stones have been prized, and even sought after as artworks. Stones and their arrangement (*ishigumi*) form the skeletal structure of the garden.

TYPES OF STONE

1 Tall Vertical

2 Low Vertical

3 Thrusting Stone

4 Reclining Stone

5 Flat Stone

You will need to pay great attention to the selection of the stones for the garden. Each stone should be selected with a purpose and position in mind. Stone arrangement is regarded as the most challenging and demanding of all the skills required as a garden creator. You can practise by arranging small stones (gathered from the wayside, garden borders and so on) in a sand tray. This is an excellent way of sharpening the eye and developing the all-important 'feel' for the placement of stones.

Types of stone

For the purposes of this book, stones may be divided into five basic categories, as listed below. These categories should be used as a general guide only, because in the final analysis the stones are used for their inherent expressive qualities, which are unique to each one. The choice of stone for a particular scheme will also be influenced by considerations of the overall mood of the garden, as well as factors such as cost and availability.

1 A Tall Vertical is a stone that is set upright, and is generally over 90cm (3ft) in height. Its verticality is pronounced. A stone of this category is often used as the 'Principal' stone of an arrangement (see page 26).

2 A Low Vertical rarely exceeds 90cm (3ft) in height, is strongly vertical, and is used in a supporting role.

3 A Thrusting Stone has a pronounced inclination of energy moving diagonally across it. The movement may be from left to right, or from right to left.

4 A Reclining Stone is a recumbent form, with emphasis on its horizontal aspect. The stone may sometimes be physically quite large. By its nature, it is a passive stone.

5 A Flat Stone is used in a practical manner, as a stepping stone, a viewing stone or a bridge. Although it takes on a humble posture, it should be borne in mind that such a stone lifts and supports the viewer.

Moving stones

Getting stones delivered to the front of your house is relatively simple, but moving the stones from there to their eventual resting position requires forethought and planning. As a general rule, stones that 'don't look too difficult to shift' when viewed in a quarry or rock yard become 'How on earth am I going to shift that?' when they are outside your front door.

Laying down a track of wooden rollers made from rounded posts is a simple but effective way of moving a large stone over a short distance. You can guide the stone along with a crowbar. Before attempting to move the stone, ensure that there are no fingers or feet in the way. People willing to

help are very useful to the operation, but utmost care needs to be taken in regard to safety. Smaller stones can be wheeled into the garden on heavy-duty sacktrucks. If you are loading small stones into a wheelbarrow, beware of your fingers. Take your time to ease the stone along in the direction you want to move it; never rush, for that is how accidents happen.

Another way of moving stones involves setting up a tripod of sturdy poles, and suspending a block-and-tackle from the apex of the triangle. By positioning the tripod forward of the centre of gravity, and in the direction you want to move the stone, as you lift

the stone it will inch forward in the desired direction. Once you have the stone where you want it, it can then be lifted off the ground if necessary to put it in its final position. This technique is commonly used in Japan for moving and positioning heavy rocks and sometimes even trees. It requires the greatest attention to safety and vigilance when in use, as it is possible to overstretch the balance and stability of the framework.

With these methods, it is possible to move and arrange stones of up to a tonne in weight, which will provide a good-sized specimen for a domestic garden. If you are really serious about

placing any stones larger than this, you will probably require heavy lifting machinery, and this will involve getting the crane into and out of the site. Whatever technique you choose for moving stones, above all take your time and carefully plan every move ahead to avoid injury.

Practicalities

If a stone needs to be transported over a lawn or soft ground, make a track of planks of wood or sheets of heavy plyboard, and ensure that the stone is moved over even surfaces.

Above left The placement of rocks is an art form, much attention is paid to their exact position.

Above right Stones are often used as the main focal point in a Japanese garden.

Parts of a stone

The 'face' of a stone is simply its most interesting aspect, taking into account the various characteristics in each category as described on page 24. The face is usually presented towards the viewer, though it may be obliquely angled away for dramatic effect. Also, the face may be partially hidden by other stones of the group, or even partially obscured by planting, to heighten the sense of suggestibility and potential. Where the stone reveals more than one face, usually the face that is best suited to the desired mood is chosen. From a single viewpoint, it is better to concentrate in this way on a single face that enhances the mood. The same stone may of course also be seen from a number of different positions, and due consideration needs to be given to the harmonization of each aspect of the design.

The part of the stone that is buried in the ground is referred to as the 'root', and it is important that the stone should have a good contact with the ground. A poorly placed stone will appear to be overbalancing, and may disturb the sensibility and sense of harmony of the viewer. The depth of the root will vary according to the requirements of the individual stone, and this should be taken into consideration when assessing the potential siting of a stone.

Right Always select a stone with its eventual positioning in mind.

Placing stones

There are a few general rules regarding the placement of stones in the garden landscape. A Tall Vertical stone is sometimes used as the 'Principal' stone in the garden, meaning that it is placed first in the sequence of setting out the arrangement, and all the subsequent stones are then placed in relation to it. In the *Sakuteiki*, the author refers to the 'requesting mood' of the stone. The placing of one stone should lead naturally to the placement of the next, and so on, until the entire arrangement is complete.

The Principal stone is often positioned in the background of an arrangement. In the *Sakuteiki*, we are warned against putting large stones near the veranda. Placing tall elements in the foreground of a composition however, has the effect of increasing the apparent depth of the scene, especially when combined with smaller elements in the distance. It may be pertinent to employ this technique of false perspective, for example, on a site where the depth is limited. Even so, it should be used with discretion, as tall, upright stones in the foreground can potentially appear overwhelming to the viewer.

Stones are best arranged in groups of uneven numbers: three, five, seven and nine are the numbers with the most positive implications. However, the type of layout you are creating will determine to a degree the nature of the stone settings. When placing the

Left Raking the gravel introduces further the idea of movement.

stones, bring the first one into position, check that the height of the stone is correct in relation to the final ground level, and that the face of the stone is in alignment with the lines of sight across the garden. When any fine adjustments have been made to the final positioning of the stone, and you are satisfied with it, ensure that the base of the stone is backfilled and the ground tamped hard around the base of the stone to secure it in position.

Stand back again and check that the stone is exactly as you want it. Once your first stone is set, use that as a guide for the placement of all the subsequent stones in its group. Each of the successive stones will need to have a relationship with the Principal stone of the group. By observing this rule as you place each of the stones in position, the group as a whole will have a cohesive and stable look to it. The stones must look as if they belong

together, and not as if they found their way together by accident.

It may be necessary to make a series of very small adjustments to the setting of a stone in order to achieve its best position. It is important to step back every now and then to consider the overall picture of the group of stones, as seen from the main viewing area, as it emerges, ensuring that every stone is necessary to the garden arrangement as a whole.

TIMBER AND BAMBOO

Both timber and bamboo are very flexible materials. Bamboo, in particular, is a common material in Japanese gardens, used for many different purposes, ranging from arches and gateways to details on a Tea House. Nearly all fencing is composed of bamboo. Timber is found mainly in the creation of structures such as arbours or pavilions.

Right Timber and bamboo are the preferred building materials in this garden. Always select materials that are suitable to the local climate.

In Japan, cryptomeria is a frequently used timber, although various types of wood may be used for Tea Houses, some of which can be ruinously expensive! With just some rudimentary skills and a little imagination, all manner of features can be incorporated in the Japanese garden.

Timber

In Japanese gardens, timber is used for a number of features, such as Tea Houses, waiting arbours and bridges. It is used for structures rather than fences, although some fences do have timber boards, and some bamboo fences sport roofs made of timber 'shingles' (wooden roofing tiles).

Timber poles can be used just as they are found – in other words, not processed into square posts or beams. For example, for a pergola carrying a wisteria over a path the uprights and cross-members could be made from natural timber poles, complete with bark. The unshaped and minimally worked timber lends a highly desirable air of rusticity. The timbers need to be carefully chosen for the purpose.

'Sleeve' fences are sections of fence, about 75–85cm (30–33in) wide and up to 1.8m (6ft) in height, which are attached to the sides of buildings as a partial screen. For example, you often see sleeve fences used in conjunction with a water basin arrangement (see page 64). Sleeve fences, although usually made of bamboo (see page 29), sometimes incorporate pieces of bent timber. When making these, particular attention should be paid to the quality of materials used and the craftsmanship of the work.

Timber posts are used as a frame on which to construct bamboo fences. The cross-members can be made of wood as well, particularly where the fence is to be of the closed screen type.

With any timber used in garden construction, make sure you use only treated timber. Gardeners in Japan scorch wood with blowtorches as a means of waterproofing it. Try to keep timber away from direct contact with the soil; in this way, it will last longer before rotting.

Bamboo

Bamboo is a material very widely used for building fences in Japanese gardens. It is also used in the detail of Tea Houses, covered seats and other garden constructions. It is possible to obtain supplies of imported bamboo, which is of a good diameter.

There are three types of bamboo fence: screen fences, see-through fences and 'sleeve' fences (see above). Screen fences are constructed from closely fitted sections of bamboo, which do not allow any sight through the fence. These are used on property boundaries for privacy. See-through fences can be employed on boundaries, or used within the garden; they can create subdivisions inside the garden space. Many kinds of fences are created in bamboo in Japan, where the material is easily available. Fences are expected to be replaced or renewed every five to eight years. Interesting variations on wooden paling fences can be made by introducing bamboo

MAKING A BAMBOO ARCH

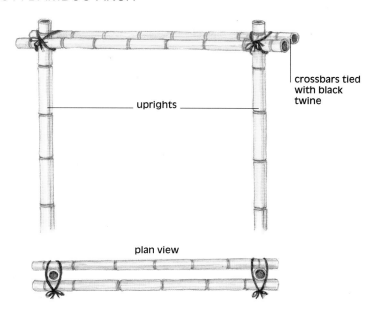

uprights

crossbars tied with black twine

plan view

verticals at intervals. Likewise, a bamboo trim on a wooden fence can set it off in an interesting way.

Bamboo archways can be erected over a path to mark a point of transition or entry into another part of the garden. Large-diameter bamboo, split carefully along its length (see below), can be used as a simple water feature.

Bamboo will not readily take stain or varnish to preserve its life outdoors. The stain is not absorbed by the coarse fibres, and varnish will quickly blister. It is better to use bamboo with the expectancy of having to replace it in

time. How long it will last will depend on the situation in which it is used. In full sun, the canes will become brittle more quickly. Try to keep the bottom of the canes off the ground, otherwise they will rot with any damp. A way to keep the canes off the ground is to lay a row of large cobbles as a base, making an attractive and practical detail (see page 77).

Below A screen fencing design for placing on a garden boundary.

Splitting bamboo poles

It is not difficult to split bamboo, but extreme care must be taken; always wear work gloves when carrying out this task. Make sure that one end of the bamboo pole is held against something solid, and make a small split with a chisel on one side. Make another split exactly opposite the first one. Carefully work the shaft of a long, heavy-duty screwdriver horizontally across and into both splits. Press down on the handle of the screwdriver on one side, while tapping the other end with a hammer on the other side. This will gradually open the split as you work down. When you get to a joint in the pole, you will have to press a little harder to work through it. Work your way very slowly and carefully, observing how the split is opening up. The grain of bamboo lies very evenly and the pole will generally split along its length as desired. Do not rush this task, but work slowly and carefully and be aware of what is happening.

GRAVEL

Gravel is most commonly used in the 'dry landscape' style of garden (*karesansui*) as a groundcover material. In general, the kind of gravel used in Japanese gardens is silvery white in colour, and consequently can bring additional light into what may otherwise be low-light areas. The spread gravel is often used in these schemes to suggest the presence of water.

There is no particular need to use one colour only. Depending on the kind of scheme being laid out, it may be possible to incorporate more than one colour; these can be laid out in interesting, flowing patterns. Generally, avoid setting the gravel shapes in a rigid pattern, and try to think more of flowing, swirling patterns which incorporate a sense of movement. Gravel areas can simply be of gravel, or ornamented with rounded cobbles laid so as to suggest watercourses. The gravel areas could also incorporate pieces of rockery stone, or even plants. Using gravel can be a way of creating a low-maintenance garden area that is also visually interesting. Gravel may also be used in paths (see page 43).

Buying gravel

Gravels are generally an inexpensive material to purchase, particularly if you use one that is local to your area. Obviously, where materials are transported over any distance cost can become a significant factor. The first place to look for gravels is in a local builder's merchant, to see what they carry as a stock item. Some merchants can supply a wide range of gravels in a variety of colours, including white and black. Always check on availability and prices, as some 'gravels' (such as crushed marble and 'spars') can be very expensive to use over large areas.

Geotextile sheeting

When using gravel as a ground-cover material, always lay a sheet of geotextile material over the surface before spreading the gravel. The sheeting is porous so it will allow water to drain away, but will not allow weeds to grow up through it from the soil below. There are various types of geotextile,

Right Simple as it is to do, gravel raking requires a steady hand. With a little imagination numerous variations can be achieved.

Practicalities

As a general guideline, a tonne of gravel will cover an area of approximately 8–10 sq m (10–12 sq yd) to a depth of 10cm (4in). This is a minimum cover; you may wish to increase the depth of gravel if you are intending to rake it into patterns once laid (see pages 48–9).

which all come in rolls and are bought by the square metre or square yard; ask at a local builder's merchant to see what they are able to supply. Do not use a non-porous sheeting for this purpose, because this may cause problems with water run-off.

Planting in gravel

It is possible to incorporate planting into gravel areas. Having laid the geotextile sheeting, decide where each plant is to grow. Then, using a sharp knife, cut a cross shape through the sheeting in each plant position, fold back the corners, and plant in the normal way. Water the plant well, and carefully fold the sheeting back around the base of the plant. This works well when planting trees, shrubs and clumps of bamboo. However, it is not recommended for herbaceous perennials, because their foliage usually dies back

in winter, which can leave the gravel looking unsightly.

Edging

Gravels are best contained within their designated areas with some sort of edging. Edging materials can include bricks, tiles on edge and timber. The choice should be in keeping with the overall mood and style of the garden scheme. Where lawns and gravel areas meet, the gravel can be retained with a timber edging; alternatively, if possible, make sure that the lawn level is a minimum of 10cm (4in) above the level of the gravel. Fine-grained gravel, where the particle size is 8mm (⅓in) or less, can be picked up on shoes and carried into neighbouring areas; so, if the gravel areas are to be walked over, it is better to provide a stepping-stone path, or other path layout, through the area for people to walk on.

Spreading and raking

Spreading the gravel in a scheme is usually one of the last tasks to be undertaken. It is best left to the end, as the gravel can become mixed with soil or other materials if it is spread earlier in the project. When laying gravel over a large area, place it in a number of evenly spaced piles before spreading it out over the entire area; this will help to ensure that an even coverage is achieved.

Raking the gravel into patterns (see pages 48–9) is another way of 'telling' visitors not to walk over it, through the power of suggestion. When they see a freshly raked gravel area, most people will think twice before disturbing the pattern with their footsteps. Young children, dogs and cats are exceptions to this, however, and will need to be treated in a sympathetic and understanding manner.

Above The raking of the gravel evokes the feeling of the movement of water.

When planning particular features for the garden, consider how they will fit into the overall garden layout. To get the best results each part of the composition should be tightly integrated into the scheme as a whole.

SPECIAL FEATURES

WATER FEATURES

Water is a very important component of the Japanese garden, because from a design point of view it implies movement. Using water is a way of both generating a sense of movement and creating a soothing atmosphere. The sound of water gently running over rocks, or falling from pool to pool, generates energy at the same time as calming the spirit.

Above The water basin is the simplest feature to arrange in a garden. Guests can use it to rinse their hands in a ritual ablution on entering the garden.

the summer months and develop algal bloom or blanket weed. Large overhanging trees will deposit quantities of leaves into a pond, which can sour the water as they rot down. Many trees in the area could also cause problems, with roots having to be cut to get any depth to the pond. So a happy medium needs to be found in terms of location. Also consider from where, and how, the pool is going to be seen and approached. A sitting area near to water is always a special place to enjoy a garden; this will need a path leading to it. If you are intending to stock the pool with fish, you will need a minimum depth of 90cm (3ft). For *koi* carp, however, a depth of 1.2m (4ft) is about the minimum required.

The simplest form of water feature is a pool in a ceramic pot or a stone water basin (see pages 50–2 and 64). A pond in the ground takes a little more work, but is usually well worth the effort, and can be used for *koi* carp or other types of fish. If you prefer to have moving water to provide sound as well as visual stimulation, you will need an electricity supply in the garden from which to run the water pump. Because of the dangers involved with electricity and water, always use a qualified electrician to install the supply. When this is done, you will be able to create anything from a simple bamboo flume trickling water into a basin (see page 64) to a complex system of waterfalls and streams (see pages 114 and 122). The

basic principles of constructing a water feature are described in the step-by-step sequences below.

Constructing a simple pool

Creating a pool in the garden is a challenge, though it is not a complicated task, and can be achieved with a little planning and some effort. Depending on the size of the pond, assistance from a mini-digger can save hours of manual digging. This can normally be hired by the day, and if access permits can certainly be helpful. Consider the size and location of the pond carefully, taking into account factors such as light levels and the presence of trees. When a pond is located in an open sunny position, it will quickly warm in

1 Make a series of trial holes across the area where you are thinking about locating the pond. This will give you an idea of the kind of material you will be digging out, such as heavy clay or lighter sandy soil. It will help you assess the nature of the task ahead.

2 Mark out the area for the pond, according to your sketch plan. Check that the edges are level, and excavate the pond area to a depth of 60cm (2ft). You can allow for an underwater shelf at this stage in the excavation of the pond. This should be at least 45cm (18in) wide, and you should allow for a minimum of 20cm (8in) depth of water over the shelf. On the shelf, you can stand baskets planted with marginal and water plants.

CONSTRUCTING A SIMPLE POOL

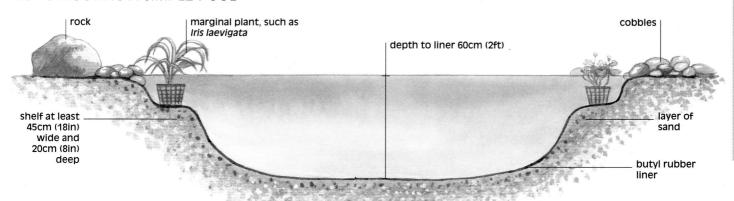

rock

marginal plant, such as *Iris laevigata*

cobbles

depth to liner 60cm (2ft)

shelf at least 45cm (18in) wide and 20cm (8in) deep

layer of sand

butyl rubber liner

3 Remove any sharp stones, and add a smooth layer of sand to the base and sides. This will help prevent the liner from becoming holed later.

4 Butyl rubber pond liners are available at water-garden stockists. To calculate the size of liner you will need, multiply the maximum length plus twice the average depth of the pond by the maximum width plus twice the average depth; this formula will give you the area required. Lay the liner carefully over the area and push it gently into the hole. Secure the liner in place with bricks around the edge.

5 Fill the pond with water run from a hose.

6 With sharp scissors, trim off the excess liner around the edge, leaving an overlap of about 15cm (6in) all the way round.

7 Disguise the liner around the edges with stones, rocks or turf. If you want a more formal edging, you could lay flat paving stones or bricks on a concrete foundation. The liner should sit on top of the concrete. Then mortar the stones or bricks into place (see page 23) on top of the liner.

Left Both still and flowing water can provide a feeling of calmness to a garden setting.

rocks to pond edge

rocks defining
island shape

topsoil

concrete to
stabilize rocks

liner

Below An island
adds mystery to a
pond. However, a
pond needs to be
fairly large in size to
accommodate an
island with planting.

Creating an island

To make an island in the pool, excavate the pool base as usual, but allow for a shallower depth where the island is to be sited. How far to excavate will depend on the size of stones you are planning to use to edge the island with, a depth of 45cm (18in) is normally enough. Plan on allowing additional space around the island before excavating further to the finished depth of the pond. Make sure that the top of the base for the island is flat and firm before spreading the liner over it. With the liner in place, very carefully bring in the stones and arrange them in sequence to create the island bank. The stones should be fitted closely together. If necessary, set their bases in concrete (see page 22) to hold them firm, but make sure no concrete is visible. When working, try to protect the liner from being punctured by laying wooden planks or boards on top of it rather than standing or kneeling directly on the liner. When the perimeter of the island is in place and secure, import topsoil 0to fill the island, firming down the soil as you go.

Making a stepping-stone path across a pool

To continue a stepping-stone path (see pages 44–5) across a pool, make sure the crossing place is no deeper than 30cm (1ft). Arrange the stepping stones in a slight arc rather than a straight line. Choose large, flat pieces of stone that will give adequate space to stand on. They should also be at least 15cm (6in) in depth, and the top of the stepping stone should rise at least 10cm (4in) above the water surface. Set the stones on pedestals built up from the bottom of the pond, using either concrete blocks or bricks. Build each pedestal to fit the particular stepping stone. Make sure that the pedestal supports cannot be seen

projecting out from under the stepping stone. Bed the stone onto the support with mortar into which a waterproofing additive has been mixed (see page 23). Ensure that the whole structure is stable, and that the tops of the stones are level.

Constructing a streamcourse

For a stream, you will need the following: a reservoir tank (such as a large plastic barrel), a standard water pump connected to an outside electricity supply, a delivery hose about 3cm (1¼in) in diameter, a butyl pond liner cut to shape, some large cobbles, hardcore, concrete and mortar, rockery stones and gravel. It is always advisable to employ a qualified electrician to install a junction box and cables in the garden. Remember that all connections to the mains supply must have a circuit-breaker. It is worth considering a double socket so that you can also run some garden lights from the supply (see pages 54–5).

1   Mark out the course of the stream. The stream bed should descend gently towards the site for the reservoir tank. Excavate the bed to a depth of 15–20cm (6–8in), and firm the base. Where the header pool and streamcourse are to be located, lay compacted hardcore to a depth of at least 15cm (6in). Check carefully that the hardcore is

well compacted, and you have removed any sharp objects which may puncture the liner, then cover the hardcore bed with a layer of sand 3.5cm (1½in) deep. The stream bed should descend gently towards the reservoir.

2   Dig a hole at the end of the stream bed, and insert the reservoir tank. Use as large a tank as you can manage, because streamcourses located in open situations are prone to water loss by evaporation on warm days. Place the pump in the reservoir tank and attach the delivery hose to the pump.

3   To form the header pool, concrete a ring of large cobbles in a pool shape at the top of the stream. Render the base with a layer of waterproof mortar (see page 23),

5cm (2in) deep. Also seal between and behind the cobbles with mortar to prevent any leakage of water. Bring the delivery hose from the pump so that it empties into the header pool. Disguise it by laying it between some of the stones, and maybe also cover it with a stone.

4   Cover the stream bed with a butyl liner, allowing plenty of overlap. Bring the liner up and into the header pool.

5   At this stage, if desired you can create low 'rills' or small dams across the stream by cementing a row of flat-topped cobbles to the bed. Ensure that the tops are level, and discreetly point between the stones, trying not to allow any mortar to show.

Above left
A stepping-stone path is an attractive way of crossing over water.

Above When creating a stream consider carefully the material to be used for the stream bed as different materials will produce different sounds and patterns.

CONSTRUCTING A STREAMCOURSE

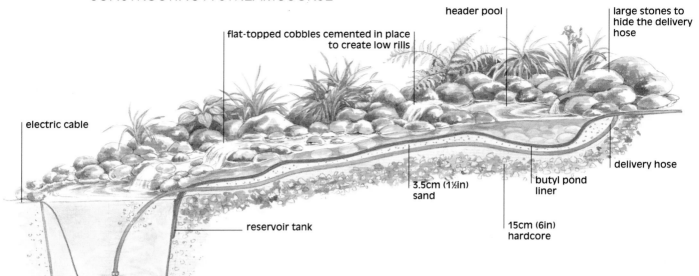

header pool

large stones to hide the delivery hose

flat-topped cobbles cemented in place to create low rills

electric cable

delivery hose

3.5cm (1½in) sand

butyl pond liner

reservoir tank

15cm (6in) hardcore

submersible pump

6 Lay a bed of concrete 10cm (4in) deep along the length of the streamcourse, starting around the base of the header pool. Arrange any rockery stones along the edge of the stream bed on top of the concrete according to your chosen design. Trim off any excess liner.

7 Arrange cobbles on the stream bed, using a variety of sizes to push the water this way and that as it winds its way downstream. Try bedding some of the cobbles into the concrete bed while it is still setting; this will create a different water pattern. Spread a thin layer of 1.5cm (½in) gravel over the stream bed, to fill in any gaps where concrete can be seen.

8 Fill the reservoir tank with water from a hose, and turn on the pump for a trial run. The header pool should fill with water and overflow into the stream. Note that when you switch off the pump the water will drain from the header pool back to the reservoir. You may have to make adjustments to the layout of the cobbles in the stream bed to create the desired flow.

Making a waterfall

A waterfall can have more than one 'step', but each one is built up in the same way. Each step is created by placing an upright 'face' stone in position, followed by its flanking stones (see page 97), working upstream, or towards the header pool if the waterfall is to come straight from there. Lay some of the offcut liner under the waterfall construction. It is best to build up the waterfall on a bed of compacted hardcore for additional stability. Finally, seal the water channel between the stones with mortar mixed with a waterproofing additive (see page 23).

Other water features

Other typical Japanese water features include a simple bamboo flume combined with a water basin (see page 64), and the bamboo 'deer-scarer', called *Shishi odoshi* in Japanese (see page 72). You can obtain one of these as a single unit from a supplier of Japanese garden artefacts. The water pumped through the spiral of copper pipe drips from the open end of the pipe onto the deer-scarer. Eventually the weight of the water causes the bamboo to fall and hit the central striking stone, making a noise. The bamboo then rises up again, and the process recommences.

Bog and iris gardens

Damp areas are difficult places to garden, if only because the access to them may at times not be easy. Creating a bog garden in which irises and other moisture-loving plants will thrive makes the most of such an area. If you do not have a naturally damp area, however, it is also possible to create a bog garden using a pond liner.

1 Mark out the outline of the area that is to be the bog garden. Choose a time when the ground is fairly dry. Decide on what is to be the final level of the soil in the bog garden and mark this with levelled pegs placed at intervals around the outline.

2 Dig out the existing soil to a depth of approximately 30cm (1ft). Make the sides of the bog garden vertical, and not gently sloping as for a pool. Ensure that the sides are level all the way round the perimeter. If you are planning the project for a large area, it will be quicker and easier to do the digging with a small excavator, if you can get one onto the site without too much difficulty.

3 Run any drains from surrounding areas into the excavated site. Lay in an additional drain to act as an overflow (see page 155), so that the bog garden will not flood during very wet weather. Set the height of the overflow pipe to a level just below the finished level of the soil. Leave a short length of the pipe projecting into the bog garden – this can be disguised with planting later on.

4 If you do not have a poorly drained subsoil, line the excavation with a pond liner (see page 35). Remove from the base of the excavation any stones or sharp objects, cover the base with a thin layer of sand,

and then spread the liner over the area. Disguise the edges with rockery stones.

5 Fill the area with fresh, good-quality topsoil, adding copious quantities of organic matter as you go – the plants will thrive on a rich soil. It is worth looking for a supplier of loam-based topsoil which is dark in colour, indicating that there is plenty of organic matter already in the soil. A peaty soil would be excellent, if available. Calculate the amount of topsoil required by roughly measuring the area of the excavation, and

multiplying by the average depth. A tonne of topsoil is approximately 0.7 cubic metres (31 cubic yards). Lightly compact the topsoil as you spread it out.

6 Plant with irises or other moisture-loving plants, such as *Primula florindae*, *Hosta elegans*, *Rodgersia pinnata* 'Superba' and *Schizostylis coccinea*, which can be planted in bold drifts in the damp ground. Plant the beds generously with bold foliage to create a strong statement. Ferns such as *Osmunda regalis* are also very striking and will thrive in the damp conditions.

Above The strong zigzag lines of the walkway create an interesting contrast to the softer lines of the plant forms.

Opposite The stream bed and edges should look as natural as possible.

BRIDGES

Bridges, *Hashi* or *Bashi* in Japanese, run the full range of styles from architecturally formal structures to more naturalistic constructions in stone or wood. One common misconception is that a Japanese garden must have a red bridge. This style of bridge was actually a Chinese garden motif: it was certainly seen in some of the larger Japanese gardens, but the bridges were known as 'Chinese' bridges.

Below Slab stone bridges can create strong lines in a composition. They also make good focal points.

Boating on the garden pond was a very popular activity in the larger gardens of the 9th- to 10th-century Heian period gardens, and the traditional Chinese half-moon bridge, which was also sometimes finished in red lacquer, was a popular feature of the gardens. It was also a practical design, because it allowed boating parties to float past underneath.

As well as their practical function, bridges provide important visual focal points in a composition. The effect of the line of the bridge can be used as a means of linking passages of the landscape scenery together. This is often a device used in *karesansui* or 'dry landscape' gardens, where the flat horizontality of the bridge stone contrasts with the vertical-emphasis peaks of the upright stones. One feature highlights the other in equal measure.

The style of bridge you choose should be carefully matched to the overall mood and style of the garden. If the design can incorporate a bridge, it should sit as part of the garden, not just as its main focus. Bridges are traditionally arranged with stones at each corner; these are known as 'anchor'

stones, and give a sense of visual stability to the layout. The anchor stones should project above the top surface of the bridge. Wherever possible, do not use a handrail except on the more formal style of bridges. If safety is an issue, for example the bridge crosses over water rather than gravel, seek to provide an alternative route. When fitting a bridge always take extra care to ensure that the construction is extremely stable.

Stone bridges

Large uncut stone slabs can be used for bridges; slate is a good material for this, and can be obtained in suitable shapes. A visit to a quarry will often reveal a number of suitable pieces for bridge stones. Otherwise it is possible to buy ready-fashioned bridge pieces for the purpose. When using a bridge stone in a stepping-stone path (see pages 44–5), the top of the bridge should be about 10cm (4in) above the top of the stepping stones, so place some bricks or pieces of flat stone under each end of the bridge, making sure that they are not visible as the bridge is approached.

Wooden bridges

The *Yatsu hashi*, or staggered wooden bridge (see page 100), is often found in the larger Japanese gardens, particularly spanning beds of *Iris laevigata*. The iris holds a particular place in Japanese culture, being celebrated as one of the flowers of summer. During the 9th and 10th centuries there was an Iris Festival, one of the most important of the year for members of the Imperial court. Iris and mugwort flowers were hung from houses, buildings and palanquins, and ladies wore the flowers in their hair. It was believed that the flowers would ward off evil spirits.

The *Yatsu hashi* bridge was also believed to be a safe place to cross when being pursued by a malevolent spirit. According to some folk legends, the spirits can only run in straight lines,

so the staggered layout of the bridge is one way of shaking off your pursuer. The bridge layout is more probably derived from the simple bridges that were to be found in the mountainous regions of Japan and China. Wooden planks were laid from rock to rock across swiftly flowing streams; these

bridges inspired painters, who would use them to indicate the dangerous currents of water. In the garden setting, the bridges are intended to allow the visitor a more relaxed passage. There are few pleasures as wonderful as walking right through areas of plants and flowers.

Above The stepping-stone path is positioned so as to direct the viewer's line of sight towards the wooden bridge.

One of the most important features in the Japanese garden, paths combine a practical function with an aesthetic quality. Paths lead the visitor both into and through the garden. The nature of a path can determine and influence the viewer's experience of the garden. A broad path allows you to walk along with your attention roaming the garden scenery.

Practicalities

Materials for paths can be collected from a wide variety of sources. It is worth looking around demolition and architectural salvage yards, where you can often find interesting materials. If you have the space to set aside and accumulate the materials for a path, it is worth doing so, but avoid turning part of the garden into a 'junkyard'.

Above The *sekimori ishi* is laid on a stepping-stone path to show that the path is closed. It diverts the viewer along a different path where there may be something particular to see.

A stepping-stone path, where you need to look for the next tread, will prevent your attention straying too far from the ground ahead. By changing the nature of the path, the attention of the viewer can be directed one way or another.

One detail of interest in relation to paths is the *sekimori ishi*, literally the 'boundary marker stone'. This is a rounded pebble or cobble about 8–10cm (3–4in) wide, bound with coarse black twine. You are most likely to see a *sekimori ishi* in a Tea Garden, placed on one of the paths in the centre of a stepping stone. The stone indicates that the path on which it has been placed is closed, and the use of the *sekimori ishi* is a convention of the Tea Garden that has spilled over into a wider context. A Tea Garden may have more than one path leading from the gate to the Tea House, and at certain times of the year one path may be of more interest to the viewer than another. By varying the path taken to the Tea House, the host tries to delight his or her guests.

It is worth ensuring that the foundations under a path are sound. If the paths are to receive heavy traffic, then lay and consolidate at least 15cm (6in) of hardcore; where traffic will be lighter, 10cm (4in) will suffice. Take time to achieve the best result you can, as then what you build will survive longer and look better. Plan your efforts in advance, and lay out the materials on the ground, frequently standing back and checking your progress. Always consider the section of garden you are working on in the context of the whole composition.

Paths in Japanese gardens may be generally divided into formal and informal. The type of path required for each situation needs to be assessed independently on its own merits.

Formal paths

The most formal type of path is a straight-edged, broad, flat, pavement-type of path, probably laid with stone flags. Formal paths are usually found leading to, or linking, buildings and garden entrances, but they rarely lead directly to where they are heading. Often a dogleg or other kind of break will be designed into the line of the path. The path is likely to have straight edges, often lined with stone kerbs. Where a variety of materials is used, these will appear in a repeating, regular pattern along the course of the path. Formal paths are likely to be wider than any informal paths that are present in the garden.

In grander gardens, you can sometimes see paths made up of small pebbles packed tightly together; although beautiful, this would be very expensive to emulate. Gravel is often used as a path surface, however, laid over a compacted hardcore base; with the gravel layer no thicker than 10cm (4in), it makes a practical surface. A gravel

Left When constructing paths, consider carefully the blend of materials you are intending to use.

comprising small rounded particles will remain loose and not pack down in the way that a crushed stone gravel will. Wherever gravel is used in the garden, there is a danger that it will migrate off the path into neighbouring areas. This is a hazard of using gravel, and you will need to take care with it. The type of surface will ultimately be dictated by the weight of traffic and importance of

the line of access – for example, a gravel path may not be suitable to lead visitors to the front door, but may be acceptable to lead them out into the garden from the rear of the house.

Informal paths

It is a good idea to vary the rhythm and manner of a path, and applying different treatments to the same path can

give interesting results. Informal paths are a miscellany of a wide variety of paths; they can include combinations of uncut stones with cut and shaped stones. A number of variations can be employed, the only limiting factors being the availability of materials and expense. Do not over-use an effect, as its freshness will wear off, nor apply an effect simply for the sake of it.

The edges of informal paths can be either neat, or broken and uneven. The materials will need to be harmonized, not necessarily in colour or size but to make sure that they work well together. Be creative when considering materials – millstones, stone kerb edgings, flat cobbles, old roof tiles set on edge, stone setts of various sizes and even bricks can be used. The path can also be broken up in sections by combining with stepping stones, leading to further opportunities for experimentation. Lay out the path materials on the ground before committing yourself to constructing the path, to make sure that they are suitable. Assemble the available materials, and draw out the path as a separate drawing if need be, before constructing it. Acquaint yourself thoroughly with what you want to do before starting the work. If you are working with small pieces of stone put together to make a tread, you should ensure that there is a compacted hardcore base under the path, and cement the stones into position. The most informal paths are the stepping-stone paths (see below) that consist of irregularly shaped and sized stones blended together.

Stepping stones

Stepping-stone paths came into fashion with the development of the Tea Garden from the late 16th century onwards. The Tea Masters, who were often designers of the gardens, chose the layout of the paths with tremendous attention to detail. The Tea Master Sen no Rikyu thought that a stepping-stone path should be six parts practical and four parts aesthetic. Oribe, a later Tea Master, reversed the advice, and declared that aesthetic considerations should be put before practical ones.

The stones should be fairly large, with an obvious flat top. Each stepping stone needs to be wide enough to take a foot comfortably; 40–60cm (15–24in) is the ideal width. Some stones in the

path can be considerably bigger than this, and such stones are often placed at points in the path where there are particularly interesting views, allowing visitors to stop and admire. Stepping stones may come from a variety of sources; they do not all have to be of the same stone. The stones are often soft-edged. It is also possible to use flat-bedded quarried stones, though these will be more angular.

Arrange the layout of the stones in patterns, for example three stones moving to the right, followed by two stones moving to the left. As well as zigzagging, paths can be laid out in gently or more steeply curving lines. In addition, stepping-stone paths can be strikingly effective when set out in straight lines, especially when running parallel to a building.

Take care when setting the stones that they are not too far apart; intervals of 10–20cm (4–8in) are good – much beyond that distance the interval becomes too far to walk over comfortably. Four or five stones will stretch over a distance of 1.8–2.5m (6–8ft). The height of the stones above the ground can vary, but 3.5–8cm (1½–3in) should be fine, depending upon the stone. When joining stones, do not butt two pointed parts of the stones. This will give the impression of the stones working against each other; instead the stones should be fitted together as if they had fallen off one piece. This will call for some juggling to get right, so be prepared to experiment with the layout of the path. Lay all the stones for the path out on the ground before firming them into position. As you check the position of each stone in relation to the next, imagine what the viewer of the garden will experience and see. When you are happy with the fine tuning of the layout of the path, dig each stone into the earth, taking particular care with tamping and packing the soil back in when infilling.

Stepping-stone paths can also be used very effectively as a bridge for

crossing a garden pool or stream-course (see pages 36–7).

Edges

Ways of edging a path can be as varied as the path surfaces themselves. Stone kerbs, stone setts, as either a single or double row, roofing tiles cut into strips and set on edge, timber rounds and bricks can all be used to effect. These should all be set in mortar (see page 23) to hold them firmly in position. You sometimes see lengths of bamboo hooped over to create an interesting edging to the side of paths in public spaces, where the intention is to keep the viewers on the paths and prevent them wandering across the grass. It is always important to match the path, and the type of edging used, to its setting and purpose.

Above Large-diameter gravel and stone kerbs are used as an edging to separate the path from the raked gravel area.

DECKING

Using timber decking is one way of creating a seating area from where the visitor can easily and comfortably appreciate the best views of the garden. It is relatively simple to erect; the easiest shape to construct is a simple square or rectangle with the planks lying straight across the area, but it is also possible to lay the planks diagonally, as well as make circles and ovals.

For the more complicated shapes and patterns, you will need to cut the timber neatly to fit. Always use a good-quality, treated timber; ask your local supplier for advice on the best type to use in your area. Some types of decking timber have non-slip surfaces, which can be desirable in wet weather. It is also possible to obtain ready-made panels of decking timber that can simply be laid next to each other. Remember to coat the timber with preservative at regular intervals to prevent it from rotting and thereby increase its life span.

Below Decking combines well with water, though try to avoid too many changes of level near the water's edge.

Constructing a square timber deck

Work out in detail, on a sketch plan, what items you will need for the area you wish to deck. If necessary, seek advice from your local garden centre or other supplier. For a basic area of decking, with the planks laid lengthways, you will require the following materials: timber planks, square-section timber joists, sand, concrete blocks, metal brackets, screws, nails and wood preservative. Gather all the materials together on site, along with the necessary tools: a spade, spirit level, screwdriver, hammer and clean paintbrush.

1 Mark out the area to be decked, using four of the planks. With a spade, mark around the outside of the planks.

2 Remove three of the planks. Place several joists at regular intervals at right angles to the remaining plank. Mark a 15cm (6in) wide border around each of the joists.

3 Remove the joists and plank and put them to one side. Dig out trenches for the joists to a depth of 10cm (4in). Line the bottom of each trench with a layer of sand, 5cm (2in) deep.

4 Place the concrete blocks in the trenches, one at each end and the others at regular intervals of about 1.2m (4ft). They should not touch the soil, and should stand slightly higher than the surrounding ground level. Using a plank and spirit level, make sure their tops are perfectly level.

5 Fill in the trenches with the remaining sand, and firm it well. Level it at the level of the surrounding soil.

6 Place the joists across the concrete blocks, checking they are perfectly aligned and level. Secure them at each end using metal brackets screwed into both joist and block.

7 Put the first plank across one edge of the joists, at right angles to the direction of the joists, and screw it firmly to each of the joists.

8 Repeat this for all the remaining top planks, leaving a small gap between them.

9 Fix four more planks neatly around the outside of the deck by nailing them to the sides and ends of the joists.

10 Treat with wood preservative and a coloured wood stain if desired.

CONSTRUCTING A SQUARE TIMBER DECK

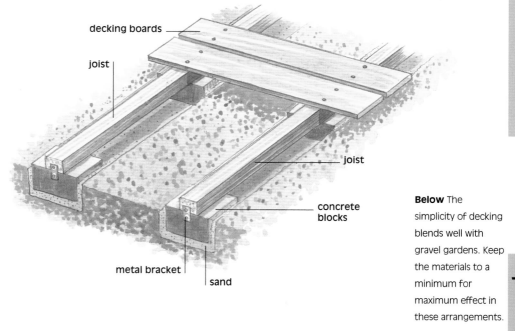

decking boards

joist

joist

concrete blocks

metal bracket

sand

Below The simplicity of decking blends well with gravel gardens. Keep the materials to a minimum for maximum effect in these arrangements.

RAKED GRAVEL

Raked patterns in sand or gravel are a distinctive feature of Japanese gardens, and this technique is used particularly in smaller, enclosed courtyard gardens. Almost invariably, the patterns are intended to evoke the spirit and feeling of the movement of water. The raking of gravel was developed into this art form by the monks of the Zen temples.

Above Gravel raking requires concentration and a steady hand.

The patterns are created by dragging a special heavy wooden rake backwards through the gravel. Freshly raked gravel has a crisp vitality, and can bring energy into what may otherwise appear to be a static design. There is ideally a balance to be found between the vigour of the raking and the dynamism of any associated rock grouping. The garden at Zuiho-in temple in Kyoto contains a garden in which there is a dynamic rock arrangement depicting a rocky shoreline being pounded by a series of heavy waves, which have been created in gravel with particularly high raked ridges.

Most often the raking is done in lines, set close to, which run horizontally across the line of sight of the viewer. This puts emphasis on the width of the garden, which is the preferred dimension of an enclosed courtyard garden. Where rocks or other features break through the gravel, a neat circle is raked around the perimeter of the feature. The gardens often occupy a space that is wider than it is deep. In such gardens, the rock arrangements and planting are often set out as a series of groupings, with the raked gravel as a means of unifying the composition. A garden in this form

will be 'read' in a similar way to rolling and unrolling a scroll painting, normally from left to right.

Gravel rakes

In Japan, gardeners use large, heavy-toothed rakes for raking gravel. This type of rake will produce a thin series of ridges and furrows in the gravel. By varying the shape of the teeth of the rake it is possible to create different patterns in the gravel. The teeth can be cut as a series of V-shapes in a plank of wood, or as a series of inverted U-shapes (see diagram below). Make the teeth at least 10cm (4in) long. Marine-grade plywood can be cut with a fretsaw to produce a rake. Draw the pattern onto the wood, making sure that you have at least 3.5cm (1½in) of timber for the width of the teeth. The width of the rake head can vary – if you have a small area of gravel, reduce the width to 75cm (30in); for larger areas, the width can be greater. Fasten the

A HOMEMADE GRAVEL RAKE

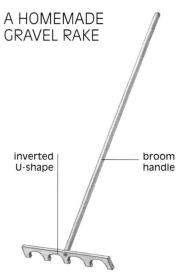

inverted U-shape

broom handle

rake head to a broom handle, and you have a simple but serviceable rake.

Raking method

Before commencing the raking, clear the gravel area of leaves and any other debris. Sweep it flat with a stiff outdoor brush. Experiment with a variety of rake patterns, and try combining different rakes to create more complex patterns in the gravel. There is an infinite number of combinations of raking patterns you can try. Rake the gravel by gently drawing the rake head backwards through it, pulling it as you move backwards. You can also vary the height of any peaks by applying differing downward pressure as you move backwards. When raking straight lines, make sure they really are parallel, as any deviance will accumulate in the pattern.

Practicalities

Plan your general movements first, so that you do not end up in the middle of a beautifully raked gravel area with no means of exit.

1 Straight-line raking

4 Winding streamcourse

7 Chequerboard

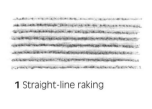

2 Straight lines alternating with waves

5 Formal wave

8 Water droplets

3 Wavy lines evoke a sense of water

6 Herringbone

9 Rough sea

STONE ORNAMENTS

Stone water basins, lanterns and pagodas are often used in Japanese gardens. The water basin, *Tsukubai*, is widely found, and is a symbol of cleansing and purity. Although the washing of hands as a symbolic act has been practised at temples for centuries, it was with the popularization of the Tea Ceremony and the Tea Garden in the 16th century that the *Tsukubai* became a common addition to gardens of all kinds.

Stone basins take numerous forms, from formally carved pieces to naturally hollowed-out stones. The significance is that the user is forced to stoop in order to use it, so adopting the position of humility – an important aspect of the preparation for the Tea Ceremony, representing a fusion of Shinto, Buddhist and Taoist elements.

Lanterns and pagodas should be placed in the garden at points where they can be seen as visual focal points in the scenery. The eye will always be drawn to a man-made structure in an otherwise naturalistic setting, and therefore the choice of siting for the feature needs to be taken with care as to its impact on the surrounding scenery. In smaller spaces, the lantern or pagoda can be displayed as the principal focal point in its own right.

Water basins

There are two types of stone water basin. The *Chozubachi* type is a tall, upright basin set adjacent to, and used from, a veranda. The *Tsukubai* or 'crouching' basin is usually set in the context of its own arrangement and does not depend on being sited within reach of a building (see page 64). It is more usually placed slightly to the side of a path, sometimes with a side path leading to the arrangement. The *Tsukubai* arrangement normally has a dense planting of shrubs to its rear, whereas the *Chozubachi* does not.

The arrangement and key elements are fairly standard. The water basin may be approached by stepping stones leading to the *Mae-ishi* or 'Front Stone', with the basin in front at

Right A waterbasin is often arranged close to the entrance of a garden or building.

Left A water basin and its attendant stone placements combine perfectly with a stone lantern. To the rear of the basin the planting should be dense and evergreen.

a comfortable arm's reach. To the left is generally a flat-topped stone, *Te-shoku-ishi*, the 'Hand Lamp Stone', on which a small portable light is placed for early-morning or late-evening ceremonies. Another flat-topped stone to the right is the *Yuto seki* or 'Hot Water Stone'; in the winter, a basin of hot water may be placed here for the guests. The gap between the *Mae-ishi* and the basin acts as a soakaway and is surfaced with an area of rounded black pebbles known as the 'Sea' (*umi*). The basin itself usually rests on a flat stone just visible beneath it. In some settings fresh water is delivered to the basin by a bamboo pipe, but it is not always required to have a supply of water pouring into the basin; the water can simply be refreshed by hand before a guest is to pass by.

With both types of basin, a bamboo dipper is laid across the top, supported by a thin, short pair of canes tied together. The space between the basin and its attendant stones is usually enclosed by edging stones or short

wooden stakes. There is no set location for a water basin arrangement, but the basin is usually placed near the entrance to the garden, or alternatively close to a building.

Lanterns

Stone lanterns (*Ishi tōrō*) are also commonly used in Japanese gardens. They

began to appear after their adoption as garden ornaments by the Tea Masters. The lanterns were first used as a means of providing lighting for Tea Ceremonies held after dark, or very early in the morning, but soon were to become used as visual focal points in the gardens. The lanterns were originally used in Buddhist temples to carry oil lights, and would have been placed in rows each side of the main entrance to the temple complex. The practice was found throughout China and Korea. There are hundreds of varieties of lantern, from the highly ornate to the rustic. The lanterns are usually carved out of stone, and they vary in size from the enormous, standing many feet high and weighing several tonnes, to small, compact shapes.

The lantern shape is derived from the form of the Indian *stupa*, a place where relics of saints were kept. The lantern comes in five sections: stem, firebox base, firebox, firebox roof and cap. The five principal parts each represent what were conceived as the components of the Universe: Heaven, Wind, Fire, Water and Earth. The lantern is composed from the three basic shapes – the triangle, the circle and the square.

Stone lanterns have always been items which the wealthy have collected for display in their gardens, and generally the more antique-looking the lantern, the more prized it is. It is now possible to obtain decent copies of stone lanterns, as they are being imported to the West from China. The better-quality lanterns have been carved from silver granite, and efforts have been made to age the stone surfaces prematurely, for example by covering them with yogurt. A brand-new lantern can look quite harshly conspicuous in a garden, and they will certainly blend in better once they have aged a little. Try standing one for a period of time in a damp, shady location; it will soon develop a patina of moss.

Pagodas

Stone pagodas (*Gorin no Tö*), are tall ornaments composed of a series of layers, or roof shapes, set on a carved stone base. They are made up of an uneven number of sections: usually 11, 13 or 15. These shapes are derived from the type of wooden building that the ancient Chinese erected in their landscape gardens, the function of which was to act as an acupuncture needle placed in the landscape at a particular point. The object of this was to facilitate the flow of harmonious and beneficial energies. The original buildings in China were made out of timber, and were highly stylized and ornate. The version which has come through to us today is altogether much simpler in design.

Below Stone pagodas are modelled after wooden buildings found in Chinese landscape gardens.

GARDEN LIGHTING

Adding lighting to the garden is a simple but highly effective way of creating additional interest in the space. It also makes the garden come alive after dark. Lighting can be introduced to the garden for several reasons: to highlight features, to create a mood, to illuminate paths and patios for use at night, and also for security.

There are two main types of lighting for the garden: downlighting and uplighting. Downlighting creates low pools of light that direct the light source downwards, and uplighting, directs the light source upwards. Uplighting is particularly useful for highlighting individual objects in the garden. When designing the lighting for a garden, make sure you are very familiar with the garden layout and its main shapes and forms. Choose among the most prominent of the features to light. Do not forget that sometimes the least expected parts of the garden can appear literally in a different light after dark. A rock arrangement is an obvious feature to light up, as is a lantern or a water feature. Likewise, a drift of grasses or a specimen bamboo can look wonderful when lit with a soft light source from near to the ground. If you are installing a water feature that will require a pump, such as a streamcourse (see pages 37–8), then you should consider installing additional capacity to run some lights at the same time.

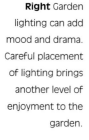

Right Garden lighting can add mood and drama. Careful placement of lighting brings another level of enjoyment to the garden.

Locating lights

Low pools of soft downlights are best located alongside paths, steps or other places where there may be a hazard to the pedestrian at night. Subtly highlighting features such as pool edges or clumps of bamboo and grasses can also be effective. Rock arrangements can look dramatic when downlit. In general, place these lights close to the ground and to the front of, or next to, the relevant feature.

Uplights, or spotlights, are better placed either behind the feature they are lighting, or at some distance away from it. Uplights directed into trees and other tall plants can create quite extraordinary effects in the night garden. Likewise, stone arrangements can be seen in strong silhouette, when uplights or spots are directed at them from behind.

Installing garden lighting

Try to plan for lighting as far ahead in the construction phase as possible if you are thinking that you may want to

Left Garden lighting can bring a focal point in the garden to life after dark.

Practicalities

It is always best to seek the advice of a properly qualified electrician regarding the availability of different types of garden lighting, and employ such a person to carry out the installation of electricity in the garden.

put lights into the garden. Roughly calculate the number and types of light you require, and note their locations. It is also possible to obtain automatic dimmer switches and timers that enable you to programme the lighting to switch on and off according to a pre-set pattern.

Any cables that are laid in the garden should be armoured, and it is best to thread the cable through a ducting for additional protection. Lay the cables at least 45cm (18in) below ground level, to prevent them being accidentally dug up. If possible, make an accurate plan of the garden indicating where the services are located. This may be useful at a later date. All connections to the mains supply must have a circuit-breaker installed.

The projects in this section are designed for small spaces, or as projects to be arranged within larger areas. As such, they should be achievable with a minimum amount of time and materials.

ONE WEEKEND PROJECTS

PATIO SINK FEATURE

Small gardens created in containers such as the old sink in this project are like living sculptures. When making one, the aim is to capture the 'feel' of a landscape, rather than to duplicate a scene in miniature. You can achieve this by considering the balance of textures and forms, and trying to develop subtle contrasts.

Shopping list

Sink or other shallow container (ideal size 75 x 60cm/30 x 24in)

Four bricks

Free-draining compost with a little added peat, enough to fill to within 8cm (3in) of top of container

One, three or five small trees such as privet, cotoneaster or Japanese holly (*Ilex crenata*)

One tall stone, about 25 x 12cm (10 x 5in)

Two smaller stones, about 15 x 8cm (6 x 3in)

Selection of alpine or other small plants such as mossy saxifrage

Alpine grit or fine gravel to cover surface of compost to a depth of 5cm (2in)

Garden moss

Tools & equipment

Drill

Trowel

Secateurs

Watering can with a fine rose

If you wish, sketch an outline plan of the principal elements within your container until you have a satisfying composition. The two main elements in our sink garden, the stones and the trees, form a roughly triangular shape, taller than it is wide, in the rear corner of the container, which is complemented by the more compact alpine plants. When siting the sink, you will need to decide on the best direction from which to view it. After positioning the stones and plants, the addition of some alpine grit or fine gravel will help define the outlines of the planted areas. It also provides a change in texture and light – in the Japanese garden, gravel often symbolizes water.

1 Choose a site that is well lit but not in direct sun. If the sink or container has no drainage holes in the base, create two or three, using a drill if necessary. Stand the container on the bricks, one at each corner, so that it is raised up off the ground to aid drainage further. Fill with compost to 8cm (3in) below the rim.

2 Following your planned layout, place the tree or group of trees (which constitute the tallest element) in position. If using more than one, ensure that the trunks do not sit one in front of the other when the sink is viewed from the chosen line of sight.

3 Place the Principal, tall stone into the arrangement, checking its alignment. When placing a stone as an upright, ensure that the stone is vertical, and not leaning to one side or the other, as this will weaken the arrangement's balance. With each new addition to the composition, step back and check that there is a connection between all the elements, and, if necessary, make fine adjustments.

4 When the tree(s) and Principal stone sit well together, add a lower stone in front and to the right. Within the overall triangular arrangement, each element of the composition should relate strongly to each of the others, all three linking into a unified whole.

5 Place the third stone on the left-hand side. Its shape should fall away to the left, and its highest point should rise towards the taller stone at the back.

6 Pack compost around the base of the stones, using the handle of the trowel, and check that the stones are stable.

Left Bonsai or shaped planting can be incorporated into sink arrangements. They also create strong focal points when placed carefully in the garden.

7 Arrange the alpines or other small plants around the base of the stones. Plant them in such a way as to suggest that the stones are rising out through the carpet of plants. Use secateurs to trim any untidy growth and make neat shapes.

8 Press pieces of garden moss into the soil, packing them closely together to form a continuous ground cover or carpet spreading out beneath the principal planting.

9 Place alpine grit or fine gravel carefully over the bare soil to a depth of 5cm (2in). When you are satisfied that everything is in place, water the whole arrangement well with a watering can with a fine rose. Any weeds that appear later should be gently teased out while they are still small.

BAMBOO TRELLIS PANEL

Bamboo is a wonderful and easy material to work with. It is versatile and has a light, elegant look. The simple but effective trellis panel described in this project makes a delightful feature for a patio or a roof garden, and you can either leave it as it is, possibly stained an interesting colour, or clothe it with twining plants.

The black twine disguises the head of the nail holding the strips together, and also provides interesting colour and texture. The design can also be adapted to fit a wide range of situations. Creating a series of frames, either the same size or in two different sizes, will allow you to mount them together in interesting patterns. If you are doing this, make the frames smaller than if there is only to be a single frame. You can also vary the size and layout of the bamboo strips to create an individual design for each panel.

1 Using the lengths of timber, saw, hammer and nails, make a sturdy square or rectangular frame that is an appropriate and practical size for your chosen space. A frame that is taller than it is wide may look better, especially if the trellis is to be a feature in its own right. Cut the ends of the timber lengths at 45°, before nailing them to each other to form a right angle.

MAKING A TIMBER FRAME

nail the two pieces of timber together

45°

45°

3.5 x 2.5cm (1½ x 1in) timber

Shopping list

Four lengths (depending on the finished panel size chosen) of 3.5 x 2.5cm (1½ x 1in) timber of a suitable grade for outdoors
Nails
Wood preservative
Bamboo strips (either ready-split bamboo obtained from a roll of split-bamboo fencing, or a piece of bamboo split into approximately 1.5cm (½in) strips)
Black twine
Screws
Wallplugs

Tools & equipment

Fine-toothed tenon saw
Hammer
Workbench
Paintbrush
Tape measure
Drill
Pencil
Screwdriver

2 Place the timber frame on a workbench (or other flat surface that is of a comfortable height to work on), and treat it with a proprietary preservative, applying at least two coats with a clean paintbrush. If the bamboo you are using is light in colour, staining the timber with a contrasting dark colour can be very effective.

3 Starting with the left-hand group of four bamboo strips, take each piece of bamboo in turn and gently curve it against the frame to fit the pattern shown here (or any other design you have chosen). Use a tape measure to check the exact length required for each strip, and then cut it to the correct length. When you are measuring, make sure that the base of each strip sits neatly on the top of the bottom section of the frame; the base of the bundle of four strips will look better if they are all properly aligned. Each successive strip should be slightly longer than the last, and they should all describe a smooth curve.

4 Drill a small-diameter hole through the base of each bamboo strip; the hole should be just large enough for the shaft of a nail and not the head. At the bottom of the frame, four strips are to be attached together, so it is important that the holes should align in order to allow one nail to pass cleanly through them all.

5 Holding each of the four bamboo strips up to the frame in turn, mark and drill another hole at the top end of the strip. The holes do not need to align here because the strips are of different lengths. On the top part of the frame, mark in pencil the position where each strip meets the frame. This will guide you later when fixing them.

6 Attach the four bamboo strips to the bottom left-hand corner of the frame first. Assemble them in their size order (number them in pencil if necessary). The smooth sides should face left; this will ensure that the smooth sides are on top when you bend them over into their final positions. Make sure the holes at the base of the four strips align. Holding the strips firmly in position, hammer a nail securely through all four strips and into the frame.

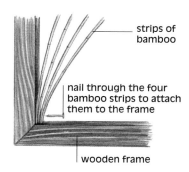

strips of bamboo

nail through the four bamboo strips to attach them to the frame

wooden frame

7 Starting with the shortest strip, bend each one over gently and attach it to the underside of the top of the frame, using the marks you made previously. Nail through the hole in each strip to attach it to the timber.

8 Turn the frame over and repeat steps 3–7. You should end up with a mirror image.

9 If desired, cover the sides of the frame by attaching further strips of bamboo (the amount needed will depend on the width of the frame) to the front face of the timber. Nail these, top and bottom, firmly into place.

bamboo strips nailed onto the frame

10 When you have completed both sides of the frame, soak the black twine in water to soften it, and then wrap a length around the base of each of the two bundles of four bamboo strips. Make sure that the wrapping turns are neat; five or six turns should be sufficient. Then tie it off tightly. Similarly, tie in each of the eight individual strips where they meet the frame; three or four turns will be sufficient here. Leaving the ends of the twine slightly long, say 2.5cm (1in), adds an interesting touch. If you do this, make sure all the knots are facing towards the front of the panel, and that all the ends are the same length.

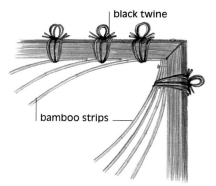

black twine

bamboo strips

11 Drill a single hole through each of the side timbers near the top. Screw the panel to the wall on each side with screws that are long enough to penetrate well into the wall, using wallplugs to make it secure. Make sure that the screw heads are flush with the surface of the frame.

DIVIDING BAMBOO FENCE

If your Japanese area is to form part of a larger garden, you will need some form of division between the two sections. This division can either completely separate off the Japanese area, or give a partial view into it without destroying the sense of enclosure.

Tools & equipment

Spade
Hammer
Paintbrush
Drill
Fine-toothed tenon saw
Pliers
Sharp knife or scissors

Shopping list

Wooden posts
Concrete (see page 22), about two bucketfuls per hole
Gravel or pieces of broken stone (four or five per hole)
Wood preservative
Wood stain (optional)
Bamboo poles, 5–8cm (2–3in) in diameter
Nails
Garden wire
Black twine
Wooden palings with rounded tops, approximately 1.2m (4ft) high (optional)
Timber rail, 5 x 3.5cm (2 x 1½in) (optional)
Screws (optional)

In this project, we create a dividing bamboo fence known in Japanese as Yotsume gaki or 'four-eyed fence', a style of fence that rarely exceeds 1.2m (4ft) in height, and usually incorporates three horizontal poles. Each pole must run truly horizontally, or the fencing will acquire a 'drunken' look that is visually unsatisfactory. You can introduce variations of your own design into several aspects of the basic style: for example, the spacing of the horizontals and verticals does not have to be exactly the same each time, but should make a consistent pattern along the length of the fence. You could also vary the heights of the verticals in a pleasing sequence. Another version of the same fencing style involves inserting wooden palings into the vertical bamboo poles. When using palings, you could close up the gaps to make the fencework less see-through, or vary the rhythm of the patterns as suggested above.

Practicalities

Bamboo poles are usually available in lengths of about 3.5m (12ft), which may be shorter than you need. To join two lengths of bamboo is easy, however. The bamboo poles have a taper, so by careful selection you should be able to slide the thick end of one pole over the thin end of the other. In this way, you can create the desired length of pole.

Left *Yotsume gaki*, or 'four-eyed' fencing, is the most common style of fencing used in the garden. The spacings between verticals can be altered to create different rhythms.

1   Plan out the fence, deciding how many sections there will be and therefore how many posts and bamboo poles you will need.

2   Set up a wooden post at each end of the fence length. Hammer the posts into the ground if they are pointed at the base. If not, dig a hole for each post and set the base in it; then backfill with concrete, adding gravel or pieces of broken stone to the mix. Make sure the tops of the posts are level to the eye. If concreting them into place, wait for the concrete to harden before proceeding. With the two end posts in position, erect posts at 2.5m (8ft) intervals between them, in the same way.

3   Treat the posts with preservative, and stain if desired (dark posts will tend to merge with the background, unless it is very light).

4   When all the support posts are in position and secure, begin to attach the horizontal bamboo poles. At each point where the horizontal pole crosses the vertical wood support post, drill through the bamboo with a fine wood drill bit, and nail through into the post.

Never nail directly through the bamboo pole, as this will result in splitting the bamboo.

5   With the saw, cut the bamboo poles that are to form the verticals to the appropriate height for the fence. Make sure that the end of the bamboo which will be at the top is cut just above a node, or bulge. Tie the vertical sections to the horizontals with garden wire in a figure-of-eight pattern, using pliers to tighten the wire as far as possible without breaking it.

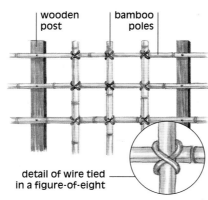

wooden post   bamboo poles

detail of wire tied in a figure-of-eight

6   Working down the length of fence, attach the black twine in a figure-of-eight pattern around each of the joints, to cover up the wire. Make sure the twine is in neat

turns around the bamboo, and keep a good tension as you work. Finish off with a knot at the front, and cut off the ends of the twine with a sharp knife or scissors, leaving about 2.5cm (1in) protruding forwards. For a variation of this, once you have made your knot wind the twine along the horizontal pole in wide, open turns to the next intersection, then tie off as before. In Japanese, this is known as *musume karage*.

7   For an alternative design for the fencework, you can use wooden palings in place of some of the bamboo verticals. Take ready-prepared palings and apply a dark wood stain. Use a timber rail for the horizontal support, and nail or screw the palings to this. Tie in the bamboo as described above.

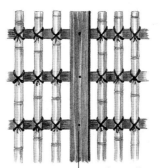

wooden palings can be interspersed with bamboo poles for an alternative design

WATER BASIN FEATURE

The stone water basin (see pages 50–52) is used in Japanese Tea Gardens for ritually washing the hands before entering the Tea House for the Tea Ceremony. The layout used in this project conforms to accepted traditional practice, and all elements of the composition fit within an overall triangular shape.

The three main stones have a designated purpose according to the conventions of the Tea Garden: the stone on the left of the basin, called the 'Hand Lamp Stone', and the one on the right, the 'Hot Water Basin Stone', should both be flat-topped; the 'Front Stone' is where one stands to use the basin, so should be wide and solid in feel. The 'Front Stone' should be a comfortable reach away from the basin. The area between the basin and the 'Front Stone' is known as the 'Sea' and is usually covered by small black pebbles. These can be difficult to find, as well as expensive, so you could try using a mixture of dark-coloured cobbles instead. Lighting up the water basin at night can create a dramatic garden feature.

Shopping list

Stone water basin (see pages 50–52)
Reservoir tank (see page 37)
Concrete (see page 22), about a wheelbarrow-full
Pond liner (see page 35), about 1.8 m (6ft) square
Flat-topped stone slabs
Geotextile sheeting (see page 30)
4 bricks or small stones
Heavy wooden plank
Large rockery stones
Cobbles of varying sizes and colours
Delivery hose (see page 37) about 2m (7ft) long
Water pump (see page 37)
Bamboo flume
Section of 'sleeve' fencing (see page 28) and two fence posts
Specimen bamboo plant
Evergreen plants such as Japanese azaleas, hostas, ferns and grasses

Tools & equipment

Hosepipe
Spade
Rake
Wheelbarrow
Spirit level
Stone-moving equipment (see pages 24–5)
Blowtorch (optional)
Trowel

1 Plan how the feature will fit into the existing garden. Mark out the area for the feature with a hosepipe. When you are happy with the shape and size, remove any lawn turf within the marked area using a spade. Roughly rake the soil level in the area of the basin, keeping any surplus soil on one side.

2 Dig a hole 15cm (6in) deep and twice the circumference of the basin. Place the reservoir tank in the hole and concrete around the top to a width of 30cm (1ft), sloping the concrete surface slightly back towards the rim of the tank. Lay the liner on top of the concrete and reservoir, making a cross-shaped cut over the top of the reservoir to allow water to drain back into the tank.

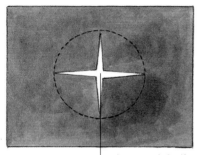

cut a cross into the liner to allow water to run back into the tank

3 Build a plinth for the basin to sit on by setting slabs of stone over the top of the reservoir. Put geotextile sheeting between liner and slabs to prevent any damage to the liner, and leave a gap between the plinth and the tank, by setting the plinth on bricks or small stones, so that you can install the pump (see step 6), and also remove it again later if necessary. When everything is set and secure, manoeuvre the basin carefully by hand onto the plinth. Using the spirit level, make sure that the top of the basin is exactly level. With a heavy basin, slide it along a heavy wooden plank to get it into position.

4 Place the attendant stones on either side so that their relationship to the basin looks natural. Ensure that the tops are level and the stones stable. It is best for the stones to be lower than the basin. Then place the 'Front Stone' in position, about 70cm (27in) from the basin and 5–8cm (2–3in) above the finished ground level.

5 Use cobbles to infill between the three principal stones, setting them in concrete. These define the extent of the basin arrangement, and also act as the 'splash zone', so any water falling within this area must be channelled back into the reservoir tank for recycling. Vary the sizes of cobbles to avoid making the encirclement of stone too regular. Place small, dark cobbles in the 'Sea' area.

6 Attach one end of the delivery hose to the pump and the other to the bamboo water flume. Place the pump in the reservoir, with the delivery hose emerging through the gap between liner and plinth. Position the bamboo flume so that it will appear to emerge from the plants slightly to one side at the rear of the arrangement. Set the bottom of the flume in concrete.

7 Position a section of 'sleeve' fencing (see page 28) behind the basin, so that some planting can be arranged between the two, as well as behind the panel. Set the fence posts in concrete (see page 23) then attach the fence section between them. To give additional interest to the fence, you could use a blowtorch (taking great care), to char the fence posts before attaching the 'sleeve' fencing.

8 Mound any surplus soil behind the basin, and plant a tall specimen bamboo immediately behind the fence panel. To highlight the basin, plant the background fairly densely with evergreens. Also plant around the base of the flume and between the stones, hiding the flexible tubing. Using plants with smaller leaves at the back and larger-leaved ones at the front gives a sense of spatial depth.

9 Fill the reservoir and basin with water. Attach the pump to an electricity supply and switch it on.

CROSS-SECTION

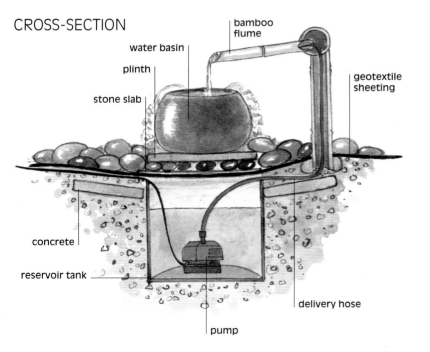

bamboo flume

water basin

plinth

stone slab

geotextile sheeting

concrete

reservoir tank

pump

delivery hose

STONE WATER BASIN AND LANTERN

In this project we combine a water basin and stone lantern in the same arrangement. There is a natural affinity between the two, and together they make a strong feature. The base of the lantern should emerge from the ground at roughly half the height of the basin when seen from the front view. The lantern with its strong vertical accent and the more horizontal basin arrangement should also describe a triangle.

Shopping list

Stone water basin arrangement
   as shown on page 64
Stone lantern (see pages 52–3)
Concrete (see page 22), a
   wheelbarrow-full
A few pieces of brick or stone
Stepping stones (optional)
Selection of plants such as privet,
   Rhododendron yakushimanum,
   evergreen azaleas, box,
   lavender and rosemary
Ornamental grasses such as
   Ophiopogon nigrescens
Cobbles of varying sizes
Leafmould or fine-grade bark
   mulch

Tools & equipment

Bamboo canes
Spade
Spirit level

Choose a lantern and water basin of similar material, so that they blend together as a unit. Choose the location for the arrangement with care. It will need to be a place to where the eye is naturally led by the shape of the garden. Also consider the background – a dense backdrop of evergreen planting is ideal, though tall mixed planting is also suitable. Decide how much space you will need – if you are building out from an existing border, the whole arrangement can be fitted into a space of 6 x 4.5m (20 x 15ft). The design as it is set out assumes you are placing it on the right-hand side of the garden, but it can be simply reversed.

1 Arrange the water basin as described on pages 64–5. It is not essential to have water pumped into the basin. If you are prepared to refresh the water on a regular basis, particularly during the warmer months, you can omit the flume, reservoir tank and pump.

2 Mound any topsoil that you excavated when levelling a base for the water basin in a gentle fashion to the rear and right of the basin, to provide a little extra height for the lantern. Once you are satisfied with the water basin arrangement, use a bamboo cane to fix the position for the lantern. Stand back and consider the scene that is emerging, and try to visualize the elements of the whole composition. Make adjustments until you are satisfied.

3 This type of lantern (see pages 52–3) is placed straight into the ground; more formal styles of lantern have a carved base to the stem. Dig a hole about 30cm (1ft) deep, and place the stem in it. Pack a small amount of concrete mix and a few pieces of brick or stone around the stem to hold it firm. With the spirit level, check that the stem is exactly vertical and the top is flat. Add the firebox base, and assemble the rest of the lantern in order. Stand back and check that all the pieces are exactly in alignment. There is no need to cement the pieces into place:the weight of the stone is sufficient.

4 If you have the space, create a section of stepping-stone path to lead up to the 'Front Stone', to draw the eye to the arrangement when it is complete.

5 Plan the siting of the main planting masses, again using bamboo canes to represent the rounded plant forms. The largest of the plant masses should be aligned to frame the lantern. Build on the triangle you created with lantern and basin. Keep stepping back to observe how each element fits in with the others, and build up the composition piece by piece. Bear in mind that the further away from

the lantern the plant shapes are, the lower and wider in shape they will appear.

6 Carry out the main planting. For each mass, try to obtain as large a plant as possible, as this will give the arrangement a more complete look from the start. If you are only able to find relatively small nursery stock, consider close planting of two or three of the same plants to make a solid clump.

7 As a highlight to the composition, add three clumps of ornamental grasses. Plant the largest clump on the right of the lantern, partially obscuring the stem, and the other two on the left.

8 Once the planting is complete, and you are satisfied that the planting and ornaments are arranged correctly, place the cobbles in a sweep across the front of the arrangement. Conceal the origin of the cobbles on the right side if possible, and likewise continue the cobbles on the left around towards the rear of the arrangement. The flow of cobbles should widen at the front of the basin, and in the space between the 'Front Stone' and the basin insert some smaller rounded cobbles.

9 Water all the plants well, and tidy the soil around them. Put a mulch of leafmould or fine-grade bark in the spaces between plants.

Left Choose a similar style of basin and lantern for this project. Creating contrast by using various foliage textures will help to bring the two elements together into a whole composition.

SMALL ZEN-STYLE GARDEN

Zen Buddhist temples developed the concept of the *karesansui*, or 'dry landscape' garden, where the presence of water is suggested rather than actual. This popular style of garden can be interpreted in many different ways. Dry, shaded conditions are some of the most difficult for garden-making, yet all is not lost.

In this project, we will transform a dry, shady corner with overhanging trees and a large holly into a quiet little haven, a place to retreat into for peace and quiet. We will create the garden to be seen primarily from in front of the existing holly tree, where we will later add a seat. The centrepiece of the arrangement is the piece of slate, on one end of which is a small lantern forming a focal point.

Shopping list

Compost suitable for planting trees and shrubs, as required
One tall, upright, smooth stone
Long, flat piece of slate
Small stone ornament (see pages 50–53)
Five rockery stones (two medium-sized, three small)
Geotextile sheeting (see page 30)
Small, rounded cobbles
Soft mortar mix (see page 23), as required
Shade-tolerant plants such as *Aucuba japonica* and *Pieris japonica*
Grasses such as *Briza media* and *Luzula sylvatica*
Ferns, including evergreens
Gravel (see page 30), as required
Bench-type or circular seat

Tools & equipment

Pruning saw
Hosepipe
Spade
Stone-moving equipment (see pages 24–5)
Sharp knife
Gravel rake (see pages 48–9) (optional)

1 Make a plan of the area, including any existing features that can be easily incorporated into the design.

2 Clear the area. Prune back over-hanging tree branches without damaging the balance of the crown (see pages 150–51). Also prune established trees to provide more light and to expose the trunk's bark.

3 Use a hosepipe to mark out a smooth, curving line to form the boundary between the new area and any existing lawn, blending the line carefully into any existing border edges. When you are happy with the composition, remove the turf and dig out the soil from the area. Level it roughly to about 10cm (4in) below the lawn level, retaining some of the best topsoil.

4 Use the retained topsoil, mixed with plenty of compost, to build up the two mounded planting areas. One is in the far right corner, and the other at the back towards the left.

5 Place the Principal stone at the front of the planting mound in the right corner. This should be a tall, upright, smooth stone with a strong outline. It should sit about 90cm (3ft) above the ground. All subsequent stones are positioned in relation to this one, and the viewing point is always from underneath the existing holly tree.

6 Arrange the piece of slate in the middle ground of the composition. On one end, place a small stone ornament as a focal point. Stand back to check the positioning.

7 Place the third stone behind the slate and adjacent to the Principal stone. It should have a smooth texture, a soft, rounded outline, and should be no higher than the 'shoulder' of the Principal. This stone creates a sense of depth.

8 Slightly to the left and in front of the slate, place a fourth stone, the outline of which falls diagonally from right to left. It is acceptable for the stone to rise a little higher than the slate; the left side of the stone should run into the ground. Move the stone gradually to the left of the slate piece until the two

stones no longer seem to have contact. Then draw the stone back slightly to the right, until it rests just at the point of losing contact with the slate. Keep checking the composition as you go.

9 Now add the three small stones, referred to as 'throwaway stones' because they are intended solely as supporting pieces. Place one to the left of the fourth stone, and one on the extreme right to support the Principal stone, yet sit a respectful distance from it – a low, rounded, large cobble (about the size of a football) would be right for this situation. The last stone goes next to the slate piece on the right; here a small, rounded stone would emphasize the opposite qualities in the slate.

10 Once you are satisfied with the arrangement, cover all the ground to be gravelled with a layer of geotextile sheeting. Cut the sheet tightly around the base of the stones with a sharp knife.

11 Arrange an area of cobbles at the edge of the planting bed from the base of the Principal stone to form

a 'headland' ending at the slate piece. Also use cobbles to define the edges of the gravel area. In the area beneath the holly tree – the viewing position – create a 'sweep' of cobbles, pushing them into some soft mortar mix to hold them firmly in place. Do not let any mortar show between the stones.

12 Plant up the two mounded areas, using the shade-tolerant plants at the rear. Keep the planting simple, using multiples of the same species in drifts. Grasses and evergreen ferns are a good choice.

13 Once everything is in place, spread gravel to a consistent depth of about 5–8cm (2–3in), or slightly deeper if you plan to rake it. You could also gravel over the path that leads to the cobbled viewing area. First cover it with geotextile sheeting, and then add a coarser gravel, perhaps of a different colour to the main gravel.

14 Add a bench seat beneath the holly tree, angled to take advantage of the best viewing position. Alternatively, place a circular seat around the trunk of the holly tree.

Above Zen gardens require a minimum of materials. The placement of, and spaces between, objects are critical. Choose materials carefully as they will be open to close visual examination.

RAISED GRAVEL BED

The idea here is to use an existing raised bed to create an interesting space that requires very little maintenance and changes with the seasons. When planning the layout of the sections within the raised bed, remember that Japanese garden design employs a 'lopsided' approach rather than perfect symmetry.

Using brick and timber for the coping will help to break up the hard lines of the walls of the bed. The dividing timbers can be stained different colours – black and dark brown set off the infilling gravel and cobbles better than bright colours. Think about the colours and textures of the pebbles and gravel. If the site has low light levels, a white gravel can uplift the space dramatically; using two or more different colours can introduce interesting contrasts. You will be able to change the planting, so you could collect a range of plants in pots for different seasons. Nearly every element can be easily altered to make either a simple change or a more radical alteration, and you can do this as often as liked.

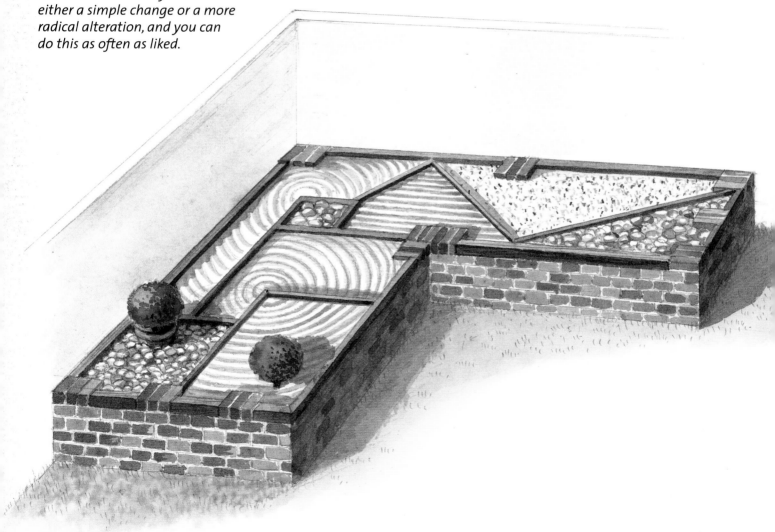

Tools & equipment

Spade
Wheelbarrow
Pointing trowel
Spirit level
Wood saw
Hammer
Sharp knife
Paintbrush
Gravel rake (see pages 48–9) or
    brush

Shopping list

Bricks for coping
Treated timber lengths, 15 x 10cm
    (6 x 4in), as required
Mortar (see page 23), as required
Wooden pegs, 2.5cm (1in) square,
    as required
Nails
Wood stain
Free-draining compost mixed
    with well-rotted garden
    compost, as required
Geotextile sheeting (see page 30)
Plants such as bamboos, grasses
    and shrubs, in large pots
Cobbles about the size of a fist
Gravel in a variety of textures and
    colours (see page 30)

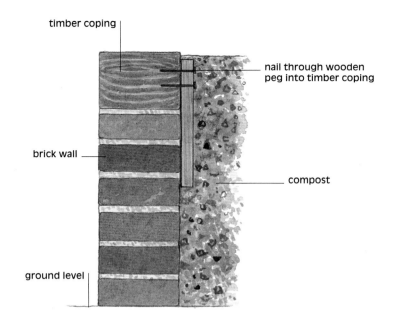

timber coping

nail through wooden
peg into timber coping

brick wall

compost

ground level

1   Remove the existing coping from
the raised bed. (If you do not have
an existing raised bed, consider
building one from scratch.)

2   Lay out the pattern of bricks and
timbers for the coping before
setting anything in place; this will
allow you to make any necessary
adjustments. Start by setting the
bricks in one corner, bedding them
on mortar, and pointing with
mortar in between. Using the spirit
level, make sure the tops are level.
Cut the first timber section to
length with the saw, and butt it up

to the bricks. Insert wooden pegs
behind the timber beam, and nail
through into the beam. The tops
of the support pegs should be at
least 3.5cm (1½in) below the top of
the beam.

3   Build the next section of brick,
followed by another timber beam.
Continue until you have worked
around the whole perimeter of the
bed. Ensure that the top is level all
the way round.

4   Fill the bed with compost, levelling
and firming it lightly to about
10cm (4in) below the top of the
coping. Lay the geotextile sheet
over the area.

5   Within the bed, lay out short
sections of timber beam to create
divisions. Since these are not to be
a permanent fixture, fix them
loosely so that they can be moved
around at a later date.

6   Arrange the potted plants in their
places. Make sure the planting
medium in the pots is enriched
with organic matter, and that it will
drain easily. Cut holes in the

geotextile sheeting with a sharp
knife and sink the pots to a
suitable level.

7   Arrange the cobble areas, using
the most interesting stones you
can find. The cobbles can all be
similar in colour and size, or mixed.

8   Fill the remaining spaces with
gravel and spread it out. The gravel
layer should reach to within 2.5cm
(1in) of the top of the dividing
timber beams.

9   Rake the gravel into patterns to
add interest to the arrangement.
Various patterns can be used, from
straight lines to swirls and circles
(see page 49). Experiment, and see
what appears. Alternatively, simply
brush the gravel until it is smooth
and flat.

Practicalities

To rake the gravel in the beds, you
could construct a shorter hand-held
version of the gravel rake described
on page 48.

WATER FEATURE WITH BAMBOO DEER-SCARER

This feature is suitable for a very small space, such as a courtyard garden. The whole layout requires a minimum area of about 1.2 x 1.2m (4 x 4ft). It sits well in a corner site, especially with brick walls as a background. The bamboo deer-scarer (*Shishi odoshi*) is available from suppliers of Japanese garden artefacts as a single unit.

The water pumped through the spiral of copper pipe drips from the open end of the pipe onto the deer-scarer. Eventually the weight of the water causes the bamboo to fall and hit the central striking stone, making a noise. The bamboo then rises up again, and the process recommences. You will need an electricity supply, so an outdoor junction box (preferably with a double socket) should be installed somewhere nearby, hidden behind plants. Japanese azaleas make ideal shrubs for background planting, complementing the specimen bamboo encircled by the copper pipe spiral. Uplighting this feature will create a dramatic focal point in the evening.

Shopping list

Specimen bamboo such as black
  bamboo (*Phyllostachys nigra*)
Organic matter, as required
Bricks (such as blue engineering
  bricks)
Mortar (see page 23), as required
Reservoir tank (big enough to
  hold three or four buckets of
  water) (see page 37)
Small square of pond liner
Piece of slate slab, or similar
Concrete (see page 22), a
  wheelbarrow-full
Water pump (see page 37)
Metal grille (optional)
Copper pipe, about 3m (10ft) long
Jubilee clip
Short length of hose
Bamboo deer-scarer
Large pebble
Evergreen shrubs (such as
  Japanese azaleas)
Junction box
Circuit-breaker
Cobbles or very coarse gravel
Low-voltage spotlights

Tools & equipment

Spade
Pointing trowel
Sharp knife
Spirit level
Pipe-bending tool (from a hire
  shop)
Screwdriver

Practicalities

CROSS-SECTION

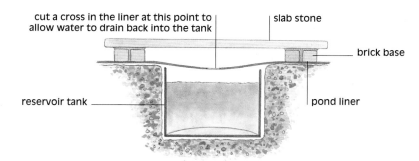

cut a cross in the liner at this point to allow water to drain back into the tank

slab stone

brick base

reservoir tank

pond liner

1 Clear the area and mark out the positions of the various elements. Work out where the finished levels are going to be: there is a brick edging at the front and sides of the feature, and the finished level of the cobbles will be just below the top of the bricks.

2 Plant the specimen bamboo plant in the far corner, incorporating plenty of organic matter into the soil. You can then build the rest of the feature around it. Lay a row of bricks around the desired area – the minimum is 1.2m (4ft) square. Lay the bricks on a bed of mortar 8cm (3in) deep, and point the gaps between the bricks neatly.

3 Dig a hole for the tank in the centre of the area. Place the tank in the hole, and backfill around it with soil, packing it down lightly as you go. Lay the pond liner over the top, with plenty of overlap to catch any water that will spill off all sides of the slab. 'Dish' the liner over the top of the tank and cut a cross through the liner, so water falling onto the sheet returns to the tank.

4 Build a brick base on each side of the reservoir tank to support the slab stone, the top of which should sit at least 10–12cm (4–5in) above the surrounding finished level. The slab stone should overlap the base on all sides, so that the base is not

showing. Concrete the slab stone to the base, using the spirit level to ensure that the top is level in all directions. Offset the angle of the slab to the front, so that it does not sit square to the line of sight.

5 Place the pump in the bottom of the tank. Put a metal grille on the opening if you wish, but do not fix it, because you may need to lift the pump for cleaning. To do this, you will have to lift the slab.

6 With the pipe-bending tool, coil the copper pipe into an open-turned spiral. Make the turns generous, and leave enough pipe to reach the deer-scarer. To hold the piece steady, pass the end of the pipe through a hole in a brick, bury the brick under the soil, and then place a neat pile of concrete over it. Pass the spiral down over the bamboo plant so that it emerges from the centre.

7 Pass a jubilee clip over the end of the copper pipe. Push the hose from the pump over the end of the pipe, which will sit below ground level. Tighten the jubilee clip over the two pipes with a screwdriver to secure them.

8 Place the deer-scarer in position and secure the 'legs' with a small amount of concrete below ground level. Align the open end of the

copper pipe and the open end of the deer-scarer. Then place the striking stone on the slab, and adjust it so that the deer-scarer hits the stone as it comes down.

9 Plant up the background with low-growing evergreen shrubs. If using azaleas, add plenty of peat, and mulch with peat every year.

10 Fill the reservoir with water, and connect and switch on the pump. Arrange cobbles loosely at the front of the feature, covering any pieces of liner that may be showing, to provide contrast in textures and colour.

11 Connect a couple of low-voltage spotlights to the socket. Use one to uplight the bamboo plant, the other to pick out the deer-scarer.

Below A deer-scarer provides a visual and aural focal point in the garden.

SIMPLE BORDER PLANTING

Although Japanese gardeners do not use borders as such, through understanding some of their basic design principles you can create interesting and different plant displays. You do not have to use plants of Japanese origin only. Many factors govern whether certain plants will grow well in a border, such as the availability of light, the acidity of the soil and the severity of winter weather.

If you are not sure which plants to choose, ask more experienced gardeners, and look around your neighbourhood to see which plants grow well. There should be an ideal proportion in the sizes and shapes of the plants in the border that can be maintained in the long term if it is to remain harmonious. Consider the textures of the plants. Japanese maples, for example, have a light, airy outline, and the foliage is not too dense, whereas many evergreens present a more solid outline. Avoid a top-heavy look by underplanting taller evergreens with delicate, feathery material. Where possible, plant in groups of three or five of the same species.

Shopping list

Selection of suitable plants for your area, including trees, shrubs, ornamental grasses and alpines
Organic matter, such as well-composted leafmould or garden compost
Plant stakes and ties (if required)
Fine-textured mulch, such as composted bark, to a depth of 8cm (3in)

Tools & equipment

Spade
Trowel
Rake or brush

1. Draw the border to scale on graph paper. Make a note of its size and what the background is like. This will aid you in determining the number of plants required and their approximate positions. When considering numbers, take into account the size of the plants available, and their likely rate of growth over several years.

2. On the scale plan, sketch out an overall structure to the border using the plant masses to represent stones. You should quickly be able to create a pleasing arrangement, but remember to take a long-term view of the 'finished' composition, as some plants will need to grow into the desired size and shape. If there are established plants in the border, decide whether they can either be included as they are or altered by pruning to fit into the scheme.

3. Prepare the ground for planting. Remove all plants that are not required. Double-dig the border to aerate the soil (see box below), and work in plenty of organic matter. If there are perennial weeds in the border, try to remove all traces, including the roots, or they will soon recolonize the area.

Left Planting is chosen mainly for its ease of sculpting and its texture. Pruning will be required to maintain a well-balanced border.

4. Without removing the plants from their pots or containers, set them out approximately in their planting positions. Stand in the place from which the composition is to be seen, and view the arrangement. Check that there is sufficient room for the plants to develop into their finished sizes. Make any adjustments while the plants are still in their pots, stepping back each time to check the effect.

5. Plant the principal elements, such as trees and shrubs, that will form the backbone of the composition. Incorporate plenty of organic matter into the planting hole, and firm the soil around the plant after it is backfilled, without compacting the soil over the roots. Leave a slight, circular depression in the soil level around the plant, as this will help to retain moisture. Stake and tie any large specimens, to prevent root disturbance if the plant rocks in the wind before it is well established.

6. When you are satisfied with the main structural elements of the planting, plant the rest of the material such as ornamental grasses and alpines to form links between them.

7. Water each plant well, tidy the soil in the whole border, and add the mulch around the plants.

Double digging

Dig out trenches 2 spits deep and turn soil from each trench into the one in front; do not mix soil from the upper and lower spits.

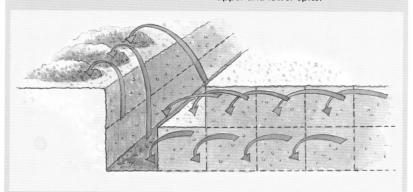

TRANSFORMING A SIDE GARDEN

The aim is to brighten up an area at the side of a house by creating a stepping-stone path through to the side gate, and providing a utility area (say for dustbins) behind a split-bamboo screen. Choose the stepping stones with care, as these will be a major feature of the layout. Make sure each one is large enough to stand on comfortably, and that the tops are reasonably flat.

Shopping list

Hardcore, as required
Mortar (see page 23), as required
Paving slabs, as required
Two timber fence posts, 8 x 8cm (3 x 3in) and 1.5m (5ft) long
Concrete (see page 22), as required
Two timber crossbars, 8 x 5cm (3 x 2in) in section
Nails or screws
Cobbles of varying sizes
Section of split-bamboo fencing (see page 29)
Coated wire
Black twine
Geotextile sheeting (see page 30)
Stepping stones
Long, flat 'bridge' stone
Four rounded 'anchor' stones to support 'bridge'
Selection of rockery stones
Two timber posts, 8 x 8cm (3 x 3in) in section, at least 1m (3½ft) long
Two bamboo poles, 10–12cm (4–5in) in diameter and 2m (7ft) long
Two bamboo poles for crossbars, 8cm (3in) in diameter, 1.2m (4ft) long
Selection of suitable plants for your area, such as azaleas and aucubas
Gravel (see page 30), as required

Tools & equipment

Spade
Spirit level
Pointing trowel
Hammer
Screwdriver
Pliers
Drill
Rake

The stones need not be of the same material or colour, but should complement one another. The stepping stones should be laid running to the left, and then to the right, and so on. When arranging stones, make sure that two complementary sides face each other. Introduce a longer slab as a 'bridge' piece in the path. The cobble 'stream' meanders, flowing under the bridge before reappearing. Place large rockery stones at the front and small ones at the back to increase the apparent depth. Arrange the planting loosely.

1 Clear and level the entire area. Make a detailed plan.

2 Lay the paving slabs for the utility area in a rectangle in front of the gate at the side of the house. First lay a compacted hardcore base at least 15cm (6in) deep. Place five spots of mortar under each slab, one at each corner and one in the centre. Then gently tap down the slab with a piece of wood until it is at the correct height. Check the paving with a spirit level. There should be a very slight fall away from the house. Some concrete slabs can be butted together, but natural stone slabs look better with the gaps pointed with mortar. Cover the paved area with a plastic sheet and keep off it for at least three days.

3 Concrete into place the two timber posts at either end of the screen (see page 23); the posts should be slightly taller than the fence panel. Nail or screw two timber crossbars to the uprights to support the fencing. At the base of the fence, concrete into place a row of large, reasonably flat-topped cobbles. This will keep the fence off the damp ground. Attach the fencing to the supports by wiring into place or by drilling through the split-bamboo canes and nailing to the crossbars. For decoration, tie some black twine at regular intervals around both crossbars.

4 Cover the remainder of the area with geotextile sheeting. Lay the stepping stones on top so that their positions can be easily adjusted. Carefully walk over the path, checking the spacing of the stones. They should sit about 5cm (2in) above ground level. When you are happy with the position of each stone, cut away the sheeting from underneath it. Then either bury the stone directly in the ground or bed it down onto a small amount of concrete. Make sure the stones are flat, and that they do not rock when walked on.

5 Place the 'bridge' stone in the path. Position the 'anchor' stones at each corner.

6 Place a low, upright rockery stone in front of the bamboo screen fence – this is the Principal stone. Then arrange the rest of the rockery stones in a loose, zigzag pattern, mimicking the stepping-stone layout, back towards the site of the arch. Frequently stand back beyond where the arch is to be, in order to get the correct viewing position. Put the tallest of the stones near the entrance.

7 Lay a loose streamcourse of rounded cobbles, mixing a variety of sizes, or grading them so that the smaller cobbles are towards the 'head' of the stream. There is no need to bed them into concrete or mortar. Continue the cobbles under the bridge if they will be seen when passing by; otherwise, arrange them to give the impression of continuing under the bridge.

8 Concrete the two timber support posts for the arch into the ground (see page 23). Sink them at least 45cm (18in) into the ground, leaving at least 60cm (2ft) to project inside the upright bamboo poles. Fit the poles over the posts, making sure they are a snug fit. Drill a hole through the bamboo on either side of each upright, and nail or screw it securely into the post. Fix the crossbars to the uprights with coated wire, and cover the wire with black twine, tied in a figure-of-eight.

9 Add the plants, with the more substantial in front of the screen and on either side of the arch.

10 Add 8cm (3in) of gravel between all the elements. Rake it level.

Above Even the smallest, most unpromising of areas can be transformed using simple, easily available materials.

SPLIT BAMBOO SCREEN

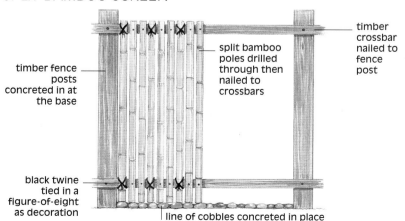

timber fence posts concreted in at the base

split bamboo poles drilled through then nailed to crossbars

timber crossbar nailed to fence post

black twine tied in a figure-of-eight as decoration

line of cobbles concreted in place

The projects outlined in this chapter are suitable for larger outdoor spaces. They develop certain ideas from Japanese gardens which can be adapted to and incorporated in our own gardens.

TWO WEEKEND PROJECTS

BORROWED LANDSCAPE

Shakkei (literally meaning 'captured alive') is an ancient technique used by garden creators in both Japan and China. It involves including, as an integral part of the composition, some element of the landscape scenery beyond the garden. In Japan, this often means mountains, but there are also examples using plains or an expanse of water.

Any object of interest outside the garden may be used, from a particularly fine view of an imposing landscape to a simple tree. To frame the view, you could use tree trunks on the garden boundary, special plantings, some part of the building from which the garden is viewed, or even the sky. You can also link the foreground of the composition to the background by using common elements. For shakkei *to work successfully, a crucial element is the manner in which the 'frame' is created and maintained; therefore, the planning stages are vitally important. You may even need to spend the whole of the first weekend planning. In our example, the 'borrowed landscape' consists of some distant rolling hills, framed by trees and shrubs already existing within the garden; your garden will inevitably be different, so try to adapt the principles outlined here to your own individual situation.*

Shopping list

Low fencing or stones for a low
    wall, if required
Trees such as *Amelanchier
    lamarckii, Betula jacquemontii,
    Crataegus* x *lavallei, Malus*
    'Profusion', *Prunus sargentii*
    and *Sorbus matsumurana*
Shrubs such as *Camellia* x
    williamsii types, *Cotinus
    coggygria, Elaeagnus* x
    *ebbingei, Osmanthus
    heterophyllus, Photinia* x
    fraseri 'Red Robin' and
    Viburnum tinus
Timber decking (see pages 46–7),
    if required
Seat
Soil for mounding
Turf or grass seed
Five pieces of rockery stone of
    suitable shapes

Tools & equipment

Spade
Pruning saw
Branch loppers
Secateurs
Rake
Stone-moving equipment (see
    pages 24–5)

1 Decide which element of the
landscape beyond the garden is
the component that you are trying
to 'capture alive'. In our example,
we have chosen to frame a view of
rolling hills in the distant
landscape. Establish the best line
of sight and the ideal viewing
position within the garden, using
photographs if necessary, and
mark these on a sketch plan (see
pages 12–15).

2 Note whether any existing gaps in
the boundary of the garden
provide the best view of the

shakkei, or whether the view could
be improved by developing a gap
further. Here, the existing garden
has a boundary that is overgrown
with trees and shrubs. Having
already made an assessment of the
best line of sight, you should now
have an idea of where and how the
gap will need to be opened up in
order to capture the view beyond.
Mark the gap on the sketch plan. If
you are starting from scratch,
decide at this stage which shrubs
and trees you wish to plant at the
sides of the view to frame the gap,
and mark these on your plan.

3 With the aid of any photographs
you have taken, consider how the
view may work in practice. One way
of helping you to do this is to place
a piece of tracing paper over a
photograph and roughly trace the
outline of the principal shapes.
Also at this stage make a note of
where the object of the view is.
With this information to hand, you
can plan how to alter what you
may already have in the garden,
and where to position any new
elements such as the grassy
mounds and rockery stones in the
foreground of our example.

Above The line of
a path can be used
to lead the viewer's
eye toward distant
scenery.

4 Think about the garden boundary. This will depend to some extent on what you already have (if anything). In this example, there is a low stone wall that will be suitable to form the 'trimming line', cutting off the lower part of the view. One of the most common ways of creating a 'trimming line' is to plant a solid hedge or build a low wall. The barrier should be solid enough to prevent gaps appearing in the framework, as this would diminish the effect you are trying to create. Another way of achieving the division is to create a change of level with, for example, a low mounding of soil, grassed over or planted with low shrubs. Mark all changes or additions on the plan. You are now ready to begin the practical work.

5 Remove carefully any plants that are directly in the planned gap. Start more or less in the centre of the gap and work a little to the left, followed by a little to the right, of the line of sight. This way there is less danger of creating too great a gap to one side or the other, and thereby losing the focus on the essential part of the landscape you are framing. When you have opened the gap enough to see through, keep stepping back to the principal viewing position to assess your progress. It is very easy to get carried away in your enthusiasm, and to find that you have opened more of a gap than is necessary or desirable.

6 Carefully prune any existing plants on each side to tidy the lines into smooth curves. This may be done with a pruning saw, branch loppers or secateurs, depending on the type and height of the plants. At each step, return to the position from which the view is to be enjoyed, checking and rechecking

that you are framing the view correctly. You will need to trim these plants on a regular basis, to prevent foliage from filling in the gap and obscuring the *shakkei*. If starting from scratch, now is the time to carry out any structural planting of trees and shrubs to complete the frame. Remember to allow for the eventual height and spread of the plants.

7 Consider the position from where the view is to be seen. This may be a simple seat placed in the garden, or it may be a more formal seating arrangement. When creating this feature, take into account the angle of view out into the landscape beyond the garden. If the position is too low, the full view will not be available to the viewer, as the boundary will cut across the line of sight. If the ground at the point where the view is to be enjoyed from is too low, it is possible to raise the viewing position by creating an area of elevated decking (see pages 46–7) on which to put a seat.

8 In this example, there are two gentle mounds in the middle ground of the composition which imitate the scenery as it appears in the background. Create these with soil, thoroughly graded with a rake, remembering that the landscaping of the mounding must be sympathetic to the general feel of the garden between the viewing position and the boundary. Therefore, if there is an extent of lawned area between the two elements, you will need to grass over the mounds with either seed or turf.

9 The final touch in this project is the small rock grouping. The hill on the right of the view is higher than the one behind it. This gives

us a pattern to follow in the arrangement of the stones. Create a grouping of five stones, placing the group of rocks on the right side of the opening. The tallest stone should be sited towards the viewing position on the nearer of the two mounds. Choose a stone that has its longest slope leaning towards the right, and the shortest, steepest slope on the left. Balance this stone with two further pieces. Place a low-lying stone behind the tall upright so that it appears to be emerging from the base of the upright. To the left of the upright, place another long, low piece; this stone should be bigger than the stone at the back, and should be placed in such a way as to support the main upright. This group of three mirrors the hill on the right in the distance. Then, on the further mound, place two other pieces of rock. The first should be a rock with a softer profile, describing a rounded triangular shape. Make sure that the height of this piece is no more than two-thirds of the height of the tall upright in the foreground. When this is in place, add its companion rock on the left. Again, this piece should be longer than it is tall, and its height should be no more than two-thirds of the height of its companion.

Above Evergreen shrubs are important elements for screening unwanted views.

Opposite The bridge acts as a linking device between the garden and the distant landscape scenery.

INFORMAL APPROACH AND ENTRANCE GATE

A Japanese garden area is intended to be a peaceful haven, detached from the everyday world, and therefore it is important to make the entrance to it special. In this project, a broad grass path leads informally towards a rustic entrance gate. As visitors approach, two planted areas project towards them, and behind these is the gate, rising above the foreground.

The grass path is obscured from the immediate view of the visitor because the two areas of the foreground are visually linked so that they appear as one piece. Only when the viewer moves closer to the foreground areas does it become evident that the grass path sweeps between the two and leads to the gate. Having reached the corner and turned towards the gate, a slight L-shaped twist in the line of the path continues to slow the approach to the gate, allowing the gate structure to act as a framing device for the garden area beyond. Giving a person time to reach their destination in this way allows them to savour the garden as it unfolds before their eyes. You could vary the design of the path by using meandering stepping stones, for example, or gravel (see pages 42–5).

Tools & equipment

Posts or canes for marking the layout
Wood saws
Hammer
Screwdriver
Spade
Tape measure
Spirit level
Stepladders
Stone-moving equipment (see pages 24–5)
Rake

Shopping list

Three timbers, 8cm (3in) square or in diameter, 1.5m (5ft) long (one for the roof ridge pole and two for the side cross-members)

Ten timbers for the roof supports, 5 x 2.5cm (2 x 1in), 65cm (26in) long

Nails and screws

At least four timber planks for the crossbars, 1.5m (5ft) long

Four treated square or rounded timber support posts, 2m (7ft) long

Two timbers, 8cm (3in) square or in diameter, 90cm (3ft) long (for the end cross-members)

Concrete (see page 22), as required

Two timbers for the vertical end supports, 5 x 2.5cm (2 x 1in), 40cm (15in) long (optional)

Slate roofing tiles, wooden roofing shingles, or thatching material (reed thatch, willow or hazel stems, or split bamboo), as required

Garden wire

Section of bamboo fencing (see page 62–3)

Topsoil, as required

Rockery stones

Structural plants, up to 2m (7ft) tall, such as *Photinia* x *fraseri* 'Red Robin'

Low-growing grasses such as *Briza media*

Low mounded plants such as *Azalea japonica*

Gravel (see page 30), as required

Broken roofing tiles or timber for edging

Above The approach to the entry gate is important as the timbers will create a framework for the elements that are arranged beyond the gateway.

1 Carefully plan the siting of the gate, fencework and garden areas which are to be created in front of the gate. The gate and the landscaped areas in the foreground should be treated as a composition in its own right. Plan it as such, only taking into account the tallest elements (probably trees) of the main garden beyond the gate which may appear as part of the scenery. The frontage of the gate should not be square on, but offset slightly to one side. Also, try not to site the gate in the centre of the scene as you approach it. Note on your plan the principal line of approach towards the gate, and this should give you the best location for the gate.

2 On the site itself, mark the best position and angle appropriate for the gateway by putting some posts or tall canes in the ground. Stand back along the line of approach and decide where to position the two mounded areas that are to form the foreground. Use short canes pushed into the ground to mark their outlines. Keep reverting to a point which will allow you to assess the composition as a whole. Do not rush into the detail, as you will lose the bigger picture of what you are creating.

3 Off site, construct the timber frame for the roof (see diagrams overleaf). Use a piece of timber 1.5m (5ft) long for the ridge pole. Screw the roof supports, at an

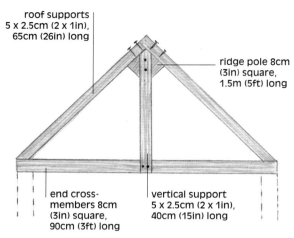

roof supports
5 x 2.5cm (2 x 1in),
65cm (26in) long

ridge pole 8cm
(3in) square,
1.5m (5ft) long

end cross-
members 8cm
(3in) square,
90cm (3ft) long

vertical support
5 x 2.5cm (2 x 1in),
40cm (15in) long

END VIEW

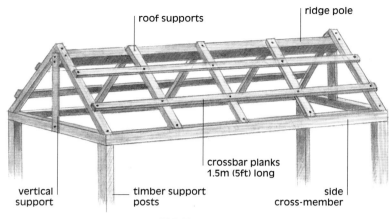

roof supports

ridge pole

crossbar planks
1.5m (5ft) long

vertical
support

timber support
posts

side
cross-member

SIDE VIEW

angle of 45°, securely to the ridge
pole, starting on one side with one
at each end of the roof. Attach
three more at regular intervals
along the length of the ridge pole.
Repeat on the other side. Then
screw the crossbar planks onto the
frame at regular intervals. If you
are using thatching material, two
on each side should be sufficient; if
using roofing tiles or shingles,
however, the crossbars should be
at intervals which allow the tiles to
be attached with a slight overlap.

4 Erect the framework for the
gateway. The posts should be
positioned to form a rectangle
1.5m (5ft) wide by 90cm (3ft) deep.
Insert the four support posts in
the ground and concrete them
into place, using a spirit level to
make sure they are perfectly
upright. Joint and screw the side
cross-members to the support
posts on both the sides and the
ends, to form the base structure
for the roof.

5 Bring the roof structure onto the
site, and lift it up onto the
framework. Stepladders and some
help will be needed at this stage.
Making sure the roof fits neatly
onto the frame, screw the 'feet' of

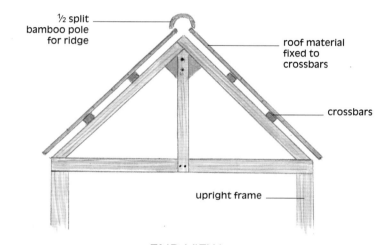

½ split
bamboo pole
for ridge

roof material
fixed to
crossbars

crossbars

upright frame

END VIEW

the roof supports onto the frame.
If desired, attach a vertical support
at each 'gable' end to give extra
strength to the structure. Once
fixed the whole structure should
be quite rigid.

6 Cover the frame of the roof with
the chosen roofing material; this
could be tiles, shingles or
thatching material. Tiles or shingles
give the structure a more formal
look. Nail or screw roof tiles or
shingles to the crossbars so that
they overlap slightly. If using willow
or split bamboo, run the lengths of
the material from the apex of the
roof towards the eaves, rather
than horizontally across the roof.

Fix thatching material or bamboo
to the roof by threading wire
through it and around the frame
timbers. You could then secure
strips of bamboo, split in half
lengthways, across the roof to
create a neat and attractive finish,
if liked.

7 Erect a section of bamboo fencing
(see pages 64–5) on each side of
the gate, attaching the panels to
the upright posts of the gate. How
much fencing to use is a matter of
taste and the space you have
available. Try to match the style of
the fence to that of the gate. If,
for example, you are using willow
as a roofing material for the gate,

you could use bundles, 8–10cm (3–4in) thick, of willow stems as part of the fencework, alternating the bundles of willow with the bamboo uprights.

8   Once the gate and fence are in place, strip away any turf from the two foreground areas; and start to build up the mounds with topsoil. The front of the left-hand area and the rear of the right-hand area are to be elevated. Raising the soil level 30–45cm (12–18in) will be enough. The idea is to create a partial screen effect once the plants have been put in place. You are trying to achieve a two-tone effect, where half of the area is raised and planted and the other half is flat, covered with gravel and raked level.

9   Arrange the rockery stones on the raised banking you have created.

There should be a relationship between the arrangement of the stones in the front and those at the back. Place an upright stone in the foreground (the Principal stone) to act as a guide for the placement of the stones in the background. Consider the two groups of stones as part of one arrangement, so that they link strongly together. Try not to make the stone arrangement too bold, since the planting is the main feature of this part of the scheme. It is a good idea to stand back along the line of approach and mark the potential positions of the plants with canes when you are planning the positioning of the groups of stones.

10 Create the main structural planting. The plants should follow the pattern dictated by the layout of stones, in a series of

overlapping triangles. Use two main plants in the foreground and one in the background. One is sited to the left of the gate, the next towards the front of the arrangement, and the third at the back. Make sure they do not visually overlap as you approach.

11 Plant drifts of low grasses between the rocks and main plant specimens. Towards the front, plant low mounds of rounded azaleas, clipped to form complementary shapes to suit the rocks and specimen plants.

12 Finally, create the flat gravel areas behind the foreground planting and on the right-hand side of the path. Rake the gravel until it is level. Define the edges of the gravel areas with timber edging, or roof tiles set on edge and firmly cemented into place.

Left The gateway acts a picture frame to the garden scenery beyond.

CRANE AND TORTOISE ISLANDS

The Crane and the Tortoise relate to the ancient Chinese legend of the 'Isles of Immortality', and are regarded in both China and Japan as symbols of good fortune. In Japan, the garden and house are traditionally very closely integrated, whereas in the West there has historically been a separation of the two.

With the advent of patio doors, however, it is now possible to create garden scenery to be seen from within. In this project, the doors are used as a 'picture frame' for the composition. Selecting suitable rocks for the 'islands' is of particular importance, with definite shapes required for specific positions. The key stones are the wing and neck stones for the Crane, and the back or shell stone for the Tortoise. While the type of rock is not crucial, it will pay dividends to spend some time researching what is available. The more local the rock the cheaper it will be. The stones do not have to be from the same source – it is more important to find stones of the correct shape.

Shopping list

Rocks of suitable shapes
Low-growing plants such as
    heathers, thymes and saxifrages
Geotextile sheeting (see page 30),
    as required
Gravel (see page 30), as required
Cobbles (optional)
Evergreen shrubs such as *Buxus
    sempervirens*, *Camellia* x
    williamsii, x *Osmarea burkwoodii*
    and *Pieris japonica* 'Firecrest'
Decking (see pages 46–7) (optional)

Tools & equipment

Spade
Rake
Stone-moving equipment (see
    pages 24–5)
Iron bar
Sharp knife

1   From inside the house, look through the patio doors to establish the angle of vision and the parameters of the view, as framed by the doors. Remember that the two rock 'islands' need to sit on a level area. You do not have to include all the area that is viewable in the design, but it is important to centre the design in that space. Here, the Crane island is located on the left as the feature is to be viewed, and the Tortoise on the right, which is the usual layout in Japanese gardens; there is no reason, however, why they cannot be reversed. The Crane island will probably be slightly longer than the Tortoise, which is

more compact. The two islands should appear to be linked. This is achieved through the use of the 'empty space' between them. You could place a flat slab of stone between the two groups, but here we are leaving it empty with a view of the background planting as the link. Linking the two groups is easier if they appear to be moving towards one another. When you have fixed the arrangement in your mind, make a detailed sketch plan of the desired layout.

2   Dig out the area for the islands, retaining any good topsoil for the background moundings. Level the area with a rake.

3   Select your pieces of stone. As this feature is located quite close to the house, it is worthwhile trying to obtain pieces as large as you can comfortably handle. It is helpful

when selecting the stones to mark them so that you can quickly tell which stones are destined for which part of the arrangement. If the feature is to be at the back of the house, use wooden rollers or other suitable stone-moving equipment to move the stones. An iron bar is a useful piece of equipment for levering the stones into their final positions.

Creating the Tortoise island

4   The shell is represented by a low, flat stone, which can be almost square in shape. Place this on a slight mound of soil, unless the stone is very deep.

5   The head stone can be a squared stone, slightly tilted; this will bring a corner up, which when placed correctly can create the look of an upturned snout. The legs are composed of short, stubby stones angled down into the ground, slightly detached from the body stone. The tail stone is usually the smallest stone.

6   It is not necessary to represent all the legs in your composition; for example, if there is not much space behind the Tortoise island you could omit the legs on the side furthest from the viewer.

THE TORTOISE ISLAND

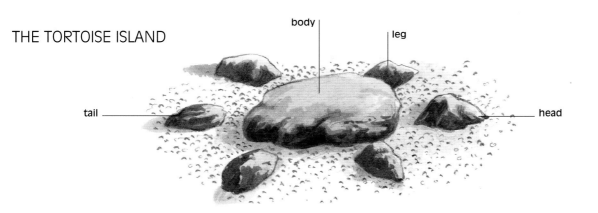

body   leg

tail   head

THE CRANE ISLAND

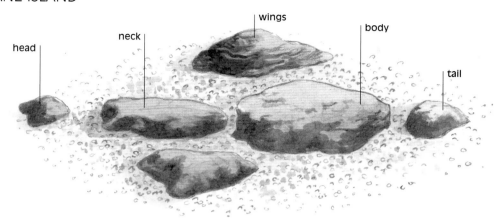

head   neck   wings   body   tail

Creating the Crane island

7 When placing the stones, take into account the depth of the gravel, which will raise the finished level of the surrounding area by 8–10cm (3–4in).

8 Begin by arranging the first of the wing stones. Keep the stone fairly square on to the frontal viewing position, to maintain and emphasize the triangular shape of the stone which is its key feature. When this is in place, put in the second wing stone behind and slightly to one side of the front wing, with a gap of about 30cm (1ft) between the two. Keep the alignment of the two stones in the same plane from the front view.

9 Put the neck stone between the wing stones, pointing away towards the right side. The neck stone should be a long, low stone, no higher than about 30–45cm (12–18in). Add the body stone to the left side of the wings; this stone should rise to no more than half the height of the wing. Add the tail stone, which should be lower again.

10 Complete the arrangement by adding the head stone, usually a low triangular piece. It is often the case that the head and tail stones are placed a little distance away from the other stones – this has the effect of elongating the overall structure. It is not necessary to be too realistic; just try to create an impression of a bird in flight. Set all the stones directly on the ground without mounding up the soil.

Planting and finishing

11 Planting in the islands should be kept to a minimum. Omit any plants in the Crane island, but use some low-growing ground-cover plants in the Tortoise. This makes an interesting contrast, though it is important to consider the background to the groups. Behind the Crane, make sure there is plenty of foliage. If the Tortoise is planted, there should be open space behind it. If the Tortoise island is raised, water drainage will be fairly quick, and it is better to plant something which will tolerate dry conditions, especially if the arrangement is in a sunny location.

12 Lay geotextile sheeting over the bare soil areas, cutting it to fit around the islands. Cover the sheeting with an even layer of gravel 8–10cm (3–4in) deep. Add bands of cobbles to create a dry 'streamcourse' if you wish, or simply rake the gravel.

13 Use any topsoil removed when creating the islands to build up background mounding behind the Crane island. You may wish to grass over the mound with either seed or turf. Alternatively, plant evergreen shrubs to create a bland, dark green background. A section of hedging, 1.2m (4ft) high, would be suitable.

14 One way of creating a smooth link between the inside of the house and the garden, if you have the space, is to fit a section of decking (see pages 46–7) outside the patio doors, at the same level as the floor inside. The decking platform should project about 1.5m (5ft) from the doors, and be slightly wider than the doors. Lay the boards of the deck so that they lead outwards from the house rather than horizontally across the line of view.

Opposite The Tortoise island in the foreground appears to be paddling his way across a gravel sea.

ABSTRACT PATIO DESIGN WITH WATER FEATURE

There is no equivalent of the patio in Japanese gardens, as the gardens are enjoyed either by walking around or from seats and buildings; but there is an element of abstraction in certain garden styles, particularly Zen gardens, where the emphasis is placed on reducing the materials to a minimum. In this project, we transform a regular patio area that can be seen from within the house.

In effect, we are creating a mosaic on the floor. A simple, bold design will have strong impact, and should be oriented in the direction from which it will most often be seen. Select your materials – maybe stones, bricks or tiles – with care, as the finished look will reflect this, and from a wide range of sources. Also think about how the material will wear. A patio surface gets varying amounts of foot traffic, and is subject to cold and damp. Ask any suppliers about which materials would be most suitable. The main design here uses slate tiles and broken paving stones to evoke the movement of water. This project also includes a cone-shaped, cobbled water feature in which the water gushes up through the centre and tumbles down the sides.

Tools & equipment

Wooden site pegs
String line
Spade
Vibrating plate compactor (from a hire shop)
Hammer
Rubber mallet
Spirit level
Watering can with a fine rose
Pointing trowel
Brush
Sharp knife
Stone-moving equipment (see pages 24–5)

1 Make a detailed survey (see pages 12–13) of the area in which you are planning to site the patio, noting not just its dimensions but also the position of drains, manhole covers, doors and windows, and if applicable any significant changes in level. Think about how the area should fall away so the rainwater will drain away from the house. Draw out the design for the

Shopping list

Hardcore material such as crushed stone or brick, as required

Filler material, such as large gravel, up to 3.5cm (1½in) in diameter, as required

Site paint

Bricks, square stone setts or kerbs, as required

Concrete (see page 22), as required

Dark-coloured slate roof tiles, as required

Dry cement mix (3 parts grit sand, 1 part cement), as required

Light-coloured broken crazy-paving stone pieces, as required

Mortar (see page 23), as required

Cement dye

Plasticizer (additive for mortar)

Sand

Large plastic plant pot

Reservoir tank

Water pump

Butyl pond liner

Delivery hose

Jubilee clip

Rounded cobbles, as required

Metal grille

Specimen shrub such as *Ilex crenata* or *Ligustrum joandrum*

Three rockery stones or two dome-shaped plants, such as azalea or box

Left The secret to good paving is the preparation of a solid foundation and taking the time to get the detail right. Blend materials to create different textures.

surface of the patio to scale. It will help later, when transferring the design to the ground, to overlay a scaled grid over the design, especially if it is complex and detailed. Detail the materials to be used in each section. Site the water feature on one side, avoiding placing it along the centre line.

2   Mark out the area with pegs and string, allowing an additional 15cm (6in) for the edging. Remove all the topsoil, excavating to a minimum depth of 20cm (8in) below the desired finished level. Build up a well-consolidated base of crushed stone or brick evenly to a depth of at least 10cm (4in). Fill in between the stones with a filler material and pack down very hard, using a vibrating plate compactor. Make sure the level of the base correctly reflects the desired finished level. Take into account the depth required for surfacing materials when preparing the foundation. If you are planning to incorporate

abstract patio design with water feature   **93**

Right Bold designs require a very careful selection of materials and a good quality of finish to the workmanship.

accurately from paper to the ground, using the site paint. Start by marking the main outlines, and once these are complete add in the smaller details.

4 Where the patio meets the garden, lay the edging. Keep it simple, so that it does not distract from the main design. Make sure the edging follows the correct levels, or pooling of water will occur. Concrete the edging material on both sides, taking care to allow enough depth on the inside for the patio surface materials.

5 Now, begin the main patio design. Bed the slate tiles on edge into a dry cement mix as closely as possible, leaving a narrow pointing gap. Run the slates in the same direction as the 'flow' of water. Try to make the edges of the slate bands as even and crisp as you can. Tamp down the slates evenly with a rubber mallet and check the levels with a spirit level. Pack the slates as tightly as you can.

6 Working your way outwards from the house walls, infill the remainder of the area with the stone pieces, carefully following the fall of the patio. Lay the stone on a mix of cement, as above, but add a little water. Tamp down each slab with the rubber mallet. Lightly sprinkle water over the whole area, and leave everything to set for at least two days before walking on the surface.

Practicalities

A useful tool for cutting and shaping stone and other hard materials is a small angle-grinder fitted with a stone-cutting disc. Great caution needs to be taken when using any power tool in the garden. Always wear a dust filter over your mouth and nose, protect your eyes with plastic goggles, and wear work gloves.

deep materials, such as large cobbles, allow a minimum of 5cm (2in) for bedding it down.

3 Peg out on the site the pattern you have overlaid on the plan, using the pegs in a grid system at about 90cm (3ft) intervals. Hammer the pegs into the ground to the correct finished heights, given the fall of the patio away from the house. This makes it easier to transfer the design

7 Point between the slates and the stones with mortar (see page 23), using a pointing trowel. Add a cement dye to the mortar, experimenting to get a colour similar to the stone – the mix will always appear darker when wet, so you will need to make allowance for this. Also add a small quantity

COBBLED FOUNTAIN

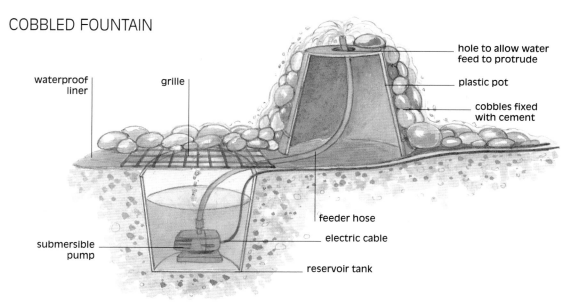

waterproof liner

grille

hole to allow water feed to protrude

plastic pot

cobbles fixed with cement

feeder hose

electric cable

submersible pump

reservoir tank

of plasticizer to the mix when applying it, smoothing the top flush with the stone surface. Brush dry sand, with a little cement mix added, into any gaps.

8 For the water feature, aim to make the finished cone about 60cm (2ft) high. Make a hole in the centre of the base of the plastic pot to allow the water feed to protrude. Dig a hole for the reservoir tank. Place the tank in the hole and put the pump into the tank. Lay out the waterproof liner over the whole

area, making sure that there is a slight gradient towards the tank. Turn the plastic pot upside down and insert the hose up through the hole in the base, making sure that it is long enough to reach the bottom of the tank. Attach the cobbles up and around the sides of the pot, packing in with a concrete mix (see page 22), leaving as small a gap as possible between each of the stones. Connect the pump to the hose with a jubilee clip, cover the top of the tank with a grille and slit the liner to allow the water

draining down to find its way into the reservoir. Use loose rounded cobbles to hide the liner.

9 Plant a specimen shrub behind the water feature; this should be grown on and trained into a windswept shape (see pages 148–9). Then add either three rocks arranged in triangular relationship to the specimen shrub, or two rounded domes of clipped azalea or box in association with the specimen shrub to make a pleasing planting composition.

Design option 2

In this slightly more detailed design, the trunk of a tree is depicted with a dark brown stone, such as Cornish slate, or a material like stoneware tiles set on edge. The foliage pads are represented by slate tiles on edge, with half-round ridge tiles cut into strips to give the tops of the pads a rounded look. The slate tiles should be trimmed to a maximum length of 20cm (8in).

BANKSIDE DRY WATERFALL

The Japanese garden tradition makes much of the idea of movement, especially to suggest the presence of water. It was in the gardens of Zen temples that the art of arranging stones to suggest islands, seas, rivers and mountains came to fruition. Today, this 'dry landscape' style, known as *karesansui*, is one of the most popular in Japan; the technique can be adapted to virtually any space and manner of interpretation.

In this project, we install a dry waterfall arrangement as a focal point in a steep but sunny bank, together with some steps and a small sitting area. Strips of mirror and dark green glass, and a 'stream' of cobbles, give the impression of water cascading down the slope, and the rocks and plants combine to create a landscape that will need little maintenance apart from routine pruning. Planting which has been shaped, or can be shaped, looks good in this situation. In Japanese gardens shaped pines are frequently used, and suitable young pine trees can often be found in nurseries. You could also install low-voltage lights to spotlight the waterfall and specimen plants and create soft pools of light for the steps.

Tools & equipment

Spade
Pointing trowel
Stone-moving equipment (see
    pages 24–5)
Hammer
Screwdriver (optional)
Paintbrushes

Shopping list

Reclaimed railway sleepers
Concrete blocks, as required
Mortar (see page 23), as required
Selection of rockery stones
Flat 'lip' stone
Strips of mirror glass and dark
    green glass
Epoxy glue
Fine granite chips
Cobbles, as required
Wooden pegs for fixing steps, as
    required
Nails or screws
Gravel (see page 30), as required
    (including some white gravel
    for the 'header pool')
Area of timber decking (see
    pages 46–7)
Wood stain and preservative
Trees for shaping, such as pines
Low rounded shrubs such as
    azaleas, box, hebes or berberis
Grasses such as *Festuca glauca*
    'Elijah Blue', *Hakonechloa*
    macra 'Alboaurea' and *Molinia*
    caerulea subsp. *caerulea*
    'Variegata' (optional)
Filler plants such as ferns and
    mosses
Reservoir tank, water pump,
    pond liner (see page 37) and
    cobbles for the bubble
    fountain (optional)
Garden lighting (see pages 54–5)
    (optional)

1   Plan the feature in detail, taking into consideration the fact that the height of the individual falls will depend on the size of stones you can manoeuvre, since the two principal flanking stones need to project above the waterfall 'lip' stone. If you really cannot face the idea of a waterfall with no water, plan to install a bubble fountain at the base of the waterfall. Allow for the steps to take the simplest route up the slope.

2   Cut the profile into the bank for the two levels of waterfall. Keep the topsoil if it is of a good quality. Dig a hole for the reservoir tank at the base of the waterfall if you are going to install a bubble fountain later. Level the area for the decking platform at the top of the slope. Put the railway sleepers in place at the bottom of the slope.

3   Build a section of concrete block wall approximately 75cm (30in) wide, either one or two courses high. Cover the face of the wall with a thin coat of mortar, making sure it is flat and even.

4   Place the first of the flanking stones, a prominent upright one, on top of one side of the block wall, slightly overlapping it at the

Above Great attention to detail is important, the alignment of the pebbles creates the effect of running water through this 'dry' stream.

front. Make sure the 'shoulder' of the stone is falling towards the centre. Place the second flanking stone on the other side of the wall, leaving a gap of at least 60cm (2ft) between the two stones; the 'shoulder' of the second stone should fall in the opposite direction. Make certain that the stones are well supported at the base and cannot fall forwards. If there are gaps between the flanking stones and the block wall, they can be filled with soil and planted later.

5   Arrange the smaller balancing stones at the sides of the two flanking stones to give the whole structure a more solid look, placing them so that they fit into the overall triangular composition.

6   Take the flat piece of stone that you have selected for the 'lip' and bed it in place with mortar. Hide any mortar that may be showing by overlapping the flanking stones to cover it.

7   Build a second course of concrete block wall to create the upper level of the waterfall, no more than two-thirds of the height of the lower fall. Above a waterfall there is usually a pool of water, so this is something that can be imitated in your construction using white gravel. Add flanking stones in the same pattern as before, but this time use slightly smaller stones. This gives the impression of the whole arrangement receding into the bank.

8   On the block wall faces which represent the sheet of water falling

Left Use garden ornaments to punctuate the planting and other aspects of the garden design.

over the 'lip', fasten strips of mirror glass and dark green glass to give the impression of water cascading down. A glass merchant will cut the pieces to size if you provide a pattern to work to. Fasten the pieces of glass to the dry wall surface with an epoxy glue. Apply a thin coat of mortar to the spaces between the pieces; while this is still tacky, press into it the fine granite chips to create a form of pebbledash.

9 Use sufficient quantities of cobbles, large and small, to simulate the watercourse, either laying them loose on the soil or bedding them in mortar (see page 23). Remember to leave a few planting pockets.

10 Now create the steps using railway sleepers, set on their sides. Fix the sleepers in place by driving in a wooden peg at the front of the sleeper at each side of the step; then nail or screw the peg to the sleeper. Disguise the pegs with rocks or plants. Place gravel on the treads of the steps.

11 Spread the topsoil that you dug out earlier over the bank to make up the finished ground levels. Take particular care to get a good depth of topsoil in the areas where trees are to be planted.

12 Create the decking area (see pages 46–7) using more railway sleepers, bedded down firmly, as a base. Make allowance for planting almost to surround the deck without obscuring the view. Stain the decking a dark colour and apply a coat of preservative.

13 Plant the specimen trees, followed by the low, rounded shrubs, and perhaps some grasses. In any gaps between the flanking stones and the wall, plant filler plants such as ferns or mosses.

14 If desired, install the bubble fountain in its position at the base of the waterfall. To do this, dig a hole for the reservoir tank approximately 45cm (18in) deep, or of a sufficient depth for the chosen reservoir tank. Place the tank in the hole and put the pump in the tank. Lay out the waterproof liner over the whole area, making sure that there is a slight gradient towards the tank. Cover the top of the tank with a grille and slit the liner to allow the water draining down to find its way back into the reservoir. Place loose rounded cobbles on top of the liner in order to hide it from view. Install the garden lighting, if desired (see pages 54–5).

BUBBLE FOUNTAIN

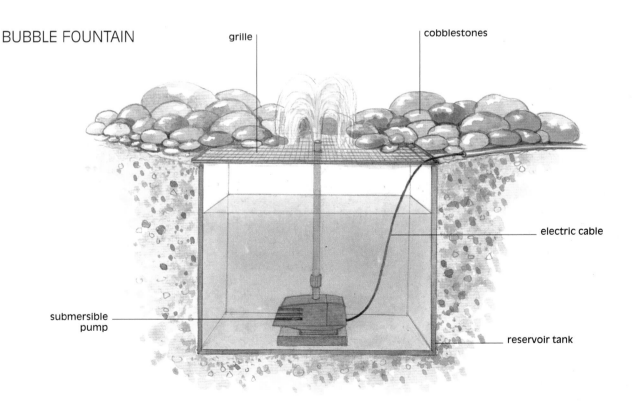

grille

cobblestones

electric cable

submersible pump

reservoir tank

IRIS GARDEN AND ZIGZAG WOODEN BRIDGE

In this garden area, the centrepiece is the bog garden (see page 39), planted principally with irises. The staggered bridge, approached via some stepping stones, allows the viewer to linger while walking at close quarters through the plants. The area is partly surrounded by raised mounds with arrangements of rocks and plants, and there is a bamboo arch marking the entrance.

This project is really for a larger garden, but it could be scaled down to fit a smaller space. There is no set length to the bridge, but here we have five sections. The two principal irises used in Japan are Iris ensata *and* I. laevigata. *The latter thrives where there is a constant water level. Towards the edges you can add drifts of* I. ensata, *as this plant prefers a slightly less damp environment. Both species have many varieties, and there should be a good choice of colours available. Irises are particularly known for deep purple-blues, as well as white. The native iris in Europe, I.* pseudacorus, *has a yellow flower, and there is also a variety with variegated foliage. Irises prefer rich soils, so ensure that the bed is mulched lightly with manure every winter.*

Shopping list

Drainpipes (see page 155), if required

Rounded timber posts, 15cm (6in) in diameter, 1.8m (6ft) long

Dark, water-repellent wood stain

Sand, as required

Pond liner (see page 35)

Hardcore, as required

Ceramic drainpipe 'sleeves', at least 30cm (1ft) long

Concrete (see page 22), as required

Walling stone, as required

Mortar (see page 23), as required

Loam-based topsoil, 1 tonne per 0.7 sq m (1 sq yd)

Organic matter, as required

Square-section rough-sawn timbers, 8 x 10cm (3 x 4in)

Bolts or heavy-duty screws ('coach' bolts)

Timber planks, 20 x 3.5cm (8 x 1½in), 2m (7ft) long

Four bamboo canes

Garden wire

Black twine

Stepping stones, as required

Three small rockery stones

Grass seed with suitable wild flower mix (optional)

Selection of irises

Tools & equipment

Wooden site pegs

String line

Spade

Small excavator (from a hire shop) for larger areas

Wood saw

Heavy mallet

Paintbrush

Thin wooden sheets

Hammer, drill or screwdriver

Spirit level

Stone-moving equipment (see pages 24–5)

Rake

1 Make a survey of the area, noting any changes of level and marking any existing trees or other plants. Dig some trial holes across the site to assess the nature of the soil; then consider whether either an overflow drain or a system to bring in water from other areas will be desirable (see page 155). Note also the direction from which you approach the area.

2 Draw up a detailed plan, including the iris garden, bridge and surrounding landscaping. The bridge here has five sections, but if space is limited you could reduce this to three. The pairs of support posts should be spaced no more than 2m (7ft) apart. The width of the crossbars should be long enough to allow for the width of the planking boards, with about 2.5cm (1in) of space either side. The support posts should project about 45cm (18in) above the planking boards.

3 Create the iris garden area as described on page 39.

4 Mark each of the rounded posts with a pencil 45cm (18in) from the top, and again 10cm (4in) below that. Cut out a section, 8cm (3in) into the post, between the marks. This will allow the crossbars to fit neatly into the joint (see step 9).

SUPPORT POSTS

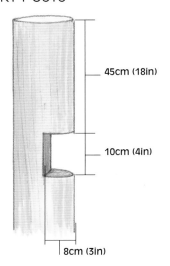

45cm (18in)

10cm (4in)

8cm (3in)

Above The zigzag bridge slows down the viewer, so allowing time to enjoy the garden at close quarters.

5 If you have a heavy clay subsoil, mark out the line that the bridge is to take with string and pegs, and hammer the bridge support posts straight into the ground with a mallet. In this case, choose posts with pointed ends, and knock them in to a depth of about 60cm (2ft) below ground level. Stain the posts, and proceed to step 8.

6 If you do not have a heavy clay subsoil, line the excavation with a thin layer of sand and a pond liner (see page 35). If your subsoil is very sandy, before laying the liner dig a trench in the ground along the line of the bridge. The trench should be the width of the bridge plus an additional 30cm (1ft) each side. Create a compacted hardcore base (to support the legs of the bridge) in the trench, at least 20cm (8in) deep, before covering with the liner. When using a liner, you can take the bridge beyond the area of the liner; thus the first and last posts can be set directly into the ground (see step 5).

7 Mark out the position of the bridge and support posts with string and pegs. In this case, use support posts with square ends to protect the liner. When installing the posts, also protect the liner by standing on thin wooden sheets. At each point where the support posts will be, insert a 'sleeve' of ceramic drainpipe into the trench, so that the top of the pipe will be at the same level as the finished level of backfilled soil. Insert the end of the post into the 'sleeve' and pack concrete around it inside the pipe. For additional support, pack pieces of walling stone and mortar around the base of each post outside the pipe. Stain the timber posts.

8 Fill the area with fresh, good-quality topsoil, adding copious quantities of organic matter. You can calculate the amount of topsoil required by roughly measuring the area of the excavation, and multiplying by the average depth. Lightly compact the topsoil as you spread it out.

9 Attach the crossbars to the support posts. Either drill right through the crossbar and post and bolt them together, or screw the crossbar to the post with a coach bolt. The two upright posts plus crossbar create a trestle, across which the planks of the bridge will span. Check that the crossbars are level using a spirit level.

FIXING CROSSBARS

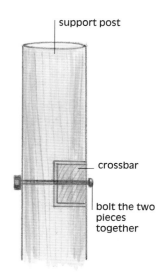

support post

crossbar

bolt the two pieces together

CROSS-SECTION OF ZIGZAG BRIDGE

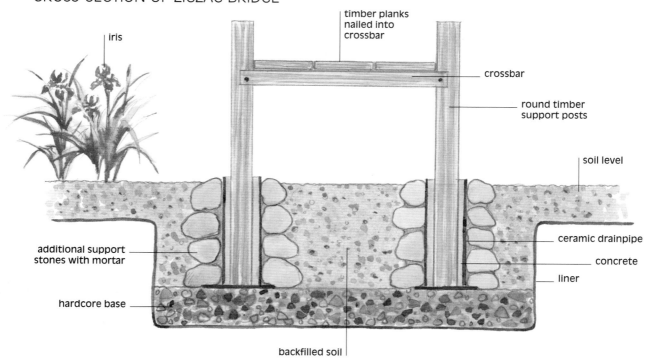

iris

timber planks nailed into crossbar

crossbar

round timber support posts

soil level

ceramic drainpipe

concrete

liner

additional support stones with mortar

hardcore base

backfilled soil

10 Lay the planking boards across the trestles, leaving slight gaps between the boards to allow for movement. Screw or nail them into the crossbars.

11 Use the soil removed when excavating the area to create the mounds to the front and rear of the iris garden. If the mound soil is poor in quality, cover it with a good depth of topsoil. Grade the line of the mounding smoothly into the existing ground levels.

12 Make a simple bamboo arch by wiring together four pieces of bamboo, and disguising the wire with black twine (see page 77). Place this in position. Lay stepping stones to take the viewer through the arch to the beginning of the bridge. The stepping stone immediately before the bridge should be a little larger than the rest, as this will encourage the viewer to pause for a moment.

13 Arrange a small group of stones on the far bank as a focal point. They should be positioned so they can be seen on the diagonal across the bed. If the area surrounding the iris bed is mainly grassed, the mounds should also be grassed. If you wish, seed the mounds with a wild flower and grass mixture for added interest.

14 Plant up the iris bed, using bold swathes of the same variety or colour. This will create more impact than intermingling different varieties, which can give a 'spotty' impression. Initially, space the plants about 45cm (18in) apart.

Right Decking walkways give the viewer the opportunity to experience the planting close at hand, creating a mood of contemplation and detachment.

Two Weekend Projects

2

BUBBLING STREAM

This feature uses the area immediately beyond a patio as a focal point, and can be enjoyed from the patio as well as from inside the house. The design creates a rising change of level towards the left-hand side of the patio, and brings a stream down over the top of the patio, flowing to the right. This can be reversed as a mirror image, if it better suits your garden layout.

The layout illustrated here provides a means of 'framing' the garden area beyond the patio, and thereby links the various components of the view together. Some elements of the background, such as tall trees or shrubs, may be worked into the plan as a whole. The addition of one strongly shaped feature shrub or tree behind the header pool is effective. The evergreen mounds contrast with drifts of softer-outlined, loosely planted grasses. The stream length is relatively short – 2.5–3m (8–10ft) is adequate – as it is the sound of the water that will be the main feature, not the stream itself. It should also be wide and shallow in profile. You will need to ensure a shallow, even fall to the stream bed at all stages of construction.

Tools & equipment

Wooden site pegs
Timber
Tape measure
Spade
Wheelbarrow
Drill and masonry bit
Pointing trowel
Sharp knife
Rake
Hose

Shopping list

Hardcore, as required

Sand, as required

Reservoir tank (see page 37), such as a large plastic barrel

Water pump (see page 37)

Delivery hose, 3cm (1¼in) diameter, as required

Butyl pond liner (see page 37), as required

Concrete (see page 22), as required

Jubilee clip

Large ceramic pot, 30cm (1ft) high

Plastic L-shaped pipe elbow

Silicone sealant

Tall, upright stone

Cobbles in a variety of sizes

Large, rounded rockery stones

Flat-topped 'lip' stone

Mortar (see page 23), as required

Waterproofing additive

Topsoil, as required

Selection of plants such as *Astilbe x arendsii* 'Bressingham Beauty', *Hebe albicans* 'Red Edge', *Hosta* 'Royal Standard', *Iris sibirica* 'Perry's Blue' and *Stipa gigantea*

Gravel, 1.5cm (½in) in diameter

1   Make a detailed survey of the existing area, noting the position of windows and doors, and the extent of the patio. It would be helpful to take a couple of photos looking out across the patio towards the rear of the garden, as you can refer to these when considering the design. Make a note of the change of level across the site; to a certain extent the gradient can be altered to suit your needs, but it is better to use and emphasize an existing slope, wherever possible. A simple way of getting an idea of the fall across the garden is to place a series of level pegs across the area, put a length of timber across the tops of the pegs, and then measure down to the ground from the timber. This will give you a good idea of the existing rise or fall in level across the site.

2   Draw up a sketch plan of the design (see pages 12–15), including all of the necessary mounding, streamcourse, placement of rockery stones and plants, and areas to be gravelled.

3   Mark out and excavate the course of the stream, allowing plenty of space for the mounding which will further refine the required fall for the stream.

Above Model your stream after natural streamcourses. Visit natural landscapes to observe such features.

HEADER POOL

ceramic pot

flanking stones

from pump

delivery hose

L-shaped pipe

4 Use the excavated soil to create the mounding. You may need to add good-quality soil if the topsoil on the site is very thin, or otherwise of poor quality. If the soil you are digging out is heavy, compact it well as you mound it. The highest point will be required in the area where the header pool is to be located. The mound should fall away to the right, almost to the original ground level, and then sweep slightly upward again. Shape the mounding and the stream-course as one piece for an harmonious result.

5 Create the stream as described on page 37, using a large ceramic pot as the header pool. Using a drill and masonry bit, carefully drill a hole in the bottom of the pot, wide enough to pass a plastic L-shaped pipe elbow through. The elbow should be of a size just narrower than the size of the delivery hose for the pump. Fix the pipe elbow into the hole at the base of the pot and seal it into place with a generous coating of silicone sealant. Allow the sealant to cure before attaching the delivery hose.

6 When the concrete on the stream bed has set, place a tall, upright stone behind the ceramic pot. The front of the stone forms the back of the header pool. If necessary, prop it in the right position using small rounded stones. Stand back on the patio to check that you have the correct position and attitude for the stone.

7 Add a rockery stone on the left of the tall, upright stone, followed by another on the right. Each of these should be placed so that there is a small gap between the pot rim and the stone.

8 Continue to add the flanking stones around the pot, finally adding the 'lip' stone, over which the water pumped back up into the header pool will overflow and cascade, at the same height as the rim of the pot.

9 Using a pointing trowel and a 3:1 mortar mix (see page 23) with a waterproofing additive mixed into it, fill in any gaps between the pot and the surrounding stones. Bring the mortar up from the base. Add further small pebbles to the rim edge if you wish.

10 Arrange further pieces of large rockery stone along the stream bed, according to your plan. Then cut the liner along the stream edge, using a sharp knife. The liner should be trimmed back to allow an upturn at the back of the stones that have just been set.

11 Bring additional topsoil in to build up the edges of the stream and to raise the soil level around the header pool stones. Complete the final shaping of the mounds.

12 Carry out the planting to suit the garden background, being fairly

Right Planting alongside a stream should be richly textured. The rounded leaves of Hostas work well with stream bank stones.

sparse with any main feature plants. The shaped mounds of accent planting are achieved by planting several small plants close together to establish the outline of the finished form. Remember to arrange the planting according to an asymmetric triangular

relationship, one of the key design concepts of a Japanese garden.

13 Add the gravel ground cover and rake it level. If the gravel borders a lawn, edge the area with an appropriate material (see page 31) to keep the gravel in place.

Above The flow of a stream can be 'fine-tuned' by the careful placement of smaller stones along its course.

These projects will require more detailed planning and forethought. By taking into account existing elements in your garden, they can be easily adapted to fit a great variety of differing situations.

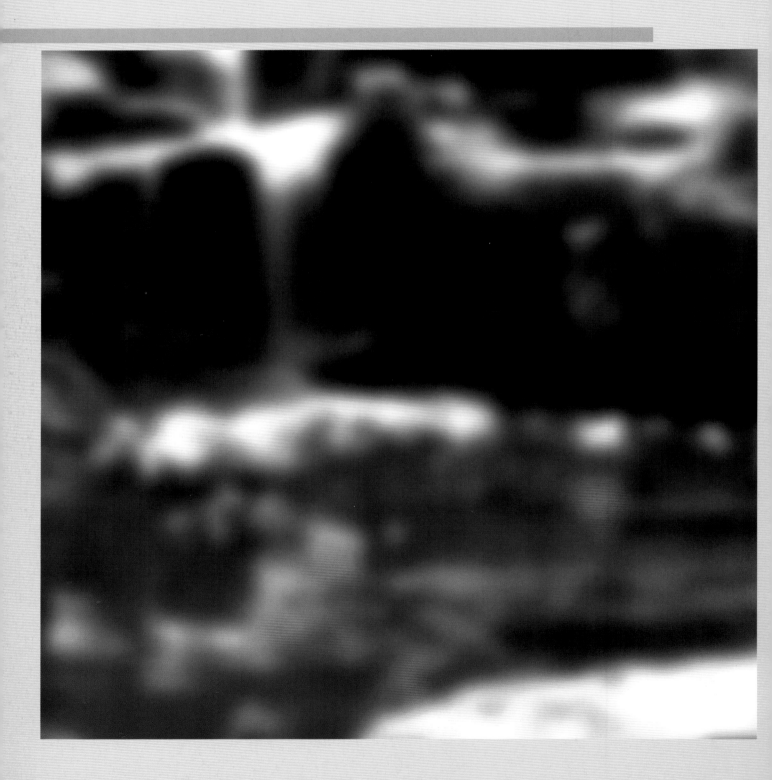

THREE WEEKEND PROJECTS

VERTICAL GARDEN

A steep slope is one of the most difficult sites to garden, but with careful thought you can use it to advantage. In this project, the face of the slope displays some strong patterns to be enjoyed from a distance, the path allows the viewer to walk through the planted area, and from the decked seating area you can see the rest of the garden from a different perspective.

The water feature adds further interest. Water is pumped up from a reservoir tank at the base of the slope to a point near the entry to the deck. It then falls from the end of a spiral piece of copper pipe over a stone into a round dish of concrete. From the bottom of the dish a drain carries the water away through a pipe along the line of the path, until it emerges above ground lower down the slope. From here the water empties into a split section of bamboo, which carries the water down the slope until it falls into a water basin at the base of the slope. When planning the planting shapes, try to create flowing lines. The lower plant shapes should have a light, floating feel, like billowing clouds drifting across the bank.

Tools & equipment

Spade
Wheelbarrow
Canes and site paint
Heavy mallet
Wood saw
Spirit level
Hammer
Screwdriver
Pipe-bending tool
Blowtorch
Sharp knife

Shopping list

Timbers for step risers, 15 x 10cm (6 x 4in), as required

Rounded wooden stakes, 8cm (3in) in diameter, as required

Crushed stone hardcore, as required

Timber posts and decking boards (see pages 46–7)

Nails and screws

Concrete (see page 22), as required

Copper pipe, 2cm (¾in) in diameter, at least 1.5m (5ft) long

L-shaped copper elbow joint

Delivery hose

Jubilee clip

Cobbles

Plastic drainpipe

Large-diameter bamboo cane, 2.5–3m (8–10ft) long

Bamboo poles

Black twine

Low, rounded stone water basin (see pages 50–2)

Reservoir tank of reasonable capacity (see page 37)

Water pump capable of delivering 1,360 litres (300 gallons) per hour (see page 37)

Rockery stones

Metal grille (optional)

Pond liner (optional)

Bamboo arch (see page 77)

Two bamboo fence panels (see page 77) (optional)

Stepping stones

Gravel (see page 30), as required

Low, mounded plants such as box or lavender

Taller-growing plants such as *Phyllostachys bissetii*, *Juniperus* 'Skyrocket', *Taxus baccata* 'Fastigiata', *Miscanthus* 'Silberfeder' or *Stipa gigantea*

Dark-coloured, fairly fine-grained mulch

Garden lighting (optional)

1 Make a survey of the site, noting the height and angle of the slope, as well as its width. Combine your on-site observations with measurements to decide on the best route for the path – ideally, it should follow the easiest incline up the slope. The entry to the path should be on one side of the site. Make a detailed plan, including any existing plants that can be retained in the new design.

2 Clear the bank of all unwanted vegetation. Mark out the route and width of the path, and the site

Above The clipped shrub forms lead the eye up the bank.

COPPER SPIRAL WATER FEATURE

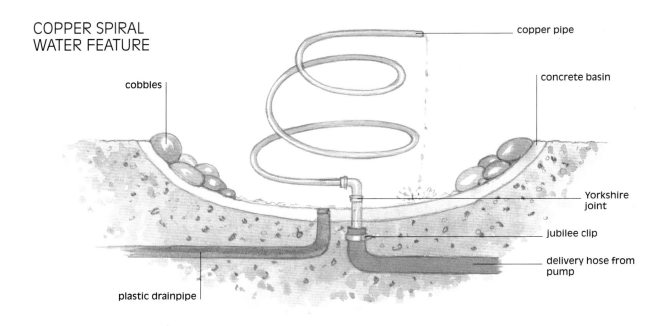

cobbles

copper pipe

concrete basin

Yorkshire joint

jubilee clip

delivery hose from pump

plastic drainpipe

Right The clipped shrubs act as a guide up the steps.

of the decking area, with canes, and spray with site paint the outlines of the principal planting areas. Stand back to check the composition, and adjust as necessary. The width of the path will vary according to the steepness of the slope; in general, the steeper the slope the narrower the path should be. A comfortable width is 75cm (30in).

3 Dig out the line of the path to a depth of about 12cm (5in), starting at the base of the slope and cutting the steps as you go along. The path can rise gently between the steps. Place the risers horizontally across the path. Using a mallet, knock a rounded stake firmly into the ground at each side of the timber riser to hold it in place. In the base of the path, build up a bed of crushed stone, compacted to a depth of 10cm (4in), leaving space for the gravel (see step 10).

4 Create the decking area at the top of the slope (see pages 46–7). This area does not have to be large: 1.8 x 2.5m (6 x 8ft) will be enough.

The front supports of the decking frame will need to be longer to allow for the slope, so set out a series of levels and string lines to determine the correct heights. Embed the base of the supports in the ground with plenty of concrete packed around them.

5 To make the copper spiral water feature, take a 1.5m (5ft) length of copper pipe, and with a pipe-bending tool fashion it into a loose spiral shape. Attach an L-shaped elbow joint to the bottom end of the spiral, and add a further straight piece of copper pipe to

the elbow. Seal the joints with a blowtorch. Attach the delivery hose to the straight pipe, and clamp it with a jubilee clip. Put the spiral in place.

6 Create a basin of concrete in a circle around the base of the spiral, and place large, rounded cobbles around the outer edge of the basin. Dish the sides of the concrete toward a length of plastic drainpipe placed in the centre. Run the drainpipe, using several sections, underground to a point near the path where it emerges above ground level.

7 Carefully split the large-diameter bamboo cane along its length into two equal halves (see page 29). Remove any membrane across the joints. Use the two sections to carry the water from the end of the drainpipe, where it emerges above ground, down the slope, arranging the bamboo, cut into appropriate sections, to follow the line of the path. Lift the bamboo chutes about 30cm (1ft) off the ground, using tripods of bamboo poles tied together with black twine, and arrange them so that the water falls from one

chute into the next as it makes its way down the slope. The water should finally fall from the last chute into the centre of the stone basin from a height of approximately 15cm (6in).

8 Create a concrete pad to drain the overflowing water from the stone basin (see diagram page 65). To do this, mark where the basin is to be located, and install the reservoir tank approximately 60cm (2ft) in front of the basin. Place the pump in the tank. Lay concrete as a base for the basin, making sure that the concrete slopes gently towards the tank. When the concrete has hardened, install the stone basin, making sure the top is level, and arranging some rockery stones around it. If you wish, you can put a metal grille over the top of the reservoir tank, and cover over the concrete with loose, rounded cobbles. You could also cover the concrete with a piece of pond liner; if you do, make sure the liner covers all of the concrete including the tank. To allow the water to run into the tank, cut a slit in the liner over the top of the tank. Fill the reservoir with water and switch on the pump to test

the flow. Make any necessary adjustments to the water feature.

9 Erect a simple bamboo arch (see page 77) near the water basin to mark the entry to the path. If you wish, you can add two short sections of fence (see page 77) on either side of the arch.

10 Place the stepping stones in position in the path. Surface the path with a 2.5cm (1in) covering of loose decorative gravel over the hardcore.

11 Plant in groups to create the desired shapes, and spread mulch in the spaces between plants.

12 If desired, place some garden lights at strategic locations. Soft pools of lights are ideal for the entry to the path, and also at key points along the path, such as corners. The water basin is an obvious feature to highlight. Uplights on the taller plants can also create interesting effects, particularly with bamboos and other plants with multiple stems.

BAMBOO CHUTES

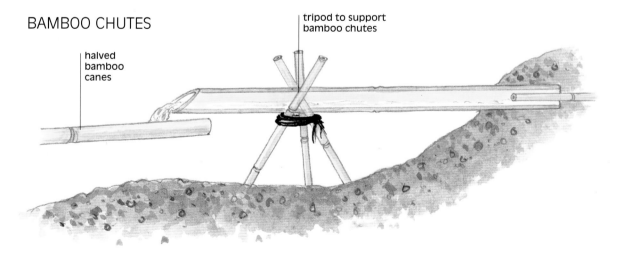

halved bamboo canes

tripod to support bamboo chutes

'SHIN' POND

The 'Shin' pond is a very old motif in Japanese garden tradition. Its shape is derived from the Chinese character meaning 'heart', 'soul' or 'spirit'. In Japanese it is called *Shin* or *Kokoro*. The very earliest Japanese gardens, which were centred on a pond and island, were attempts to make a home for the gods on earth.

The garden was intended to influence the state of mind of the viewer, and to bring a feeling of harmony with nature. In this project, the Chinese character is represented loosely, in outline only, in the shape of the pool; you should try to get the overall balance of the shape correct rather than worrying about following it exactly. The water will form a level surface, so a fall across the site will mean building up one side and having a slope cut on the other. The pond will require a deeper section, particularly if you are intending to stock fish, because they will need a minimum depth of 90cm (3ft). Think about where the excavated material is to be taken to, since it is time-consuming and costly to take it off site. Consider how the planting around the pond will fit in with the remainder of the garden.

Shopping list

- Sand or geotextile sheeting (see page 30), as required
- Pond liner (see page 37)
- Rockery stones
- Hardcore, as required
- Waterproof cement additive
- Water pump (see page 37)
- Delivery hose
- Concrete (see page 22), as required
- Concrete blocks
- Rough walling stones
- Mortar (see page 23), as required
- Bricks or flat stones
- Long, flat bridge stone
- Cobbles and gravel (see page 30)
- Stepping stones
- Timber decking (see pages 46–7) or paving slabs
- Timber fence posts, 10 x 10cm (4 x 4in)
- Timber boards, 10 x 3.5cm (4 x 1½in)
- Nails and screws
- Large-diameter bamboo canes
- Long, flat stone
- Stone lantern (see pages 52–3)
- Selection of suitable plants for your area
- Garden lighting (optional)
- Seat

Tools & equipment

- Wooden site pegs
- Site paint
- Spirit level
- Spade
- Mini-digger for large areas (from a hire shop)
- Wheelbarrow
- Pickaxe for loosening soil, if necessary
- Wooden planks for moving wheelbarrow, if necessary
- Plyboard sheets
- Pointing trowel
- Wood saw
- Hammer and screwdriver
- Rake

1 Make a brief survey of the area, marking any existing features that are to remain. Also note the levels on the site. At this stage, it is helpful to mark out the approximate outline of the pond, so that you can walk around the shoreline to get a feel for the space the water will occupy and the areas surrounding it. Plan the shape of the pond, including the island, the bridge, and the stepping stones across it. Then plan the surrounding areas. Site the sitting area with care to give the best views across the pond.

2 Using pegs and site paint, mark out the shape of the pond on the ground. Place pegs at 1.5m (5ft) intervals around the perimeter of the pond, and ensure the tops are level using a long piece of wood as a straight edge and a spirit level. This will show you where there is any building up to do.

3 Excavate the pond, either by hand digging or with a machine. Work methodically, digging out the pond in a series of layers, depending on the eventual depth, each about 20cm (8in) deep. Keep the topsoil and subsoil separately on one side, for later use (see step 4). After you have taken the surface layer off the pond, mark out the shelf for the bankside stones about 15cm (6in) below the anticipated waterline inside the pond. Cut out the shelf. Angle the sides of the pond at no greater than 30°.

4 Using the excavated soil, create the bank and the two steps for the waterfall (see page 38). With the subsoil, build up the elevations in layers, lightly compacting each time. When happy with the shape, add a layer of topsoil and firm it down. At the top of the bank, create a dish-shaped hole for the header pool.

5 Smooth out the sides and base of the pond. Check that the projected water-level line is even all the way around the top of the pond. Cover the excavation with geotextile sheeting or a layer of sand, before installing the butyl liner (see page 35). When calculating the liner size,

Left Vary bank-side textures alongside a pond as this will create interest and variation to the scenery.

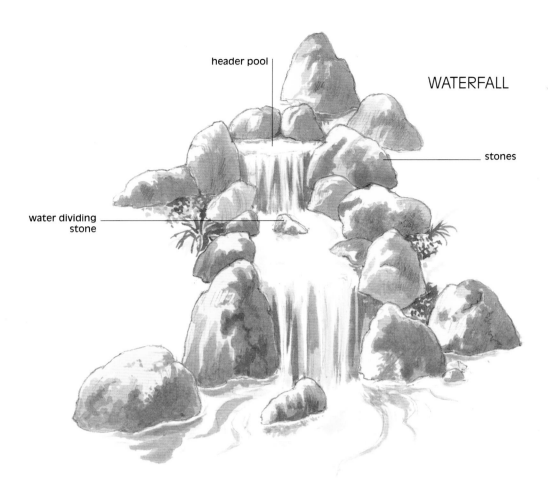

header pool

WATERFALL

stones

water dividing
stone

allow for plenty of overlap. Fill the base of the pond with water to stretch the liner. Bring the liner right up beyond the position of the stones behind the header pool of the waterfall, and secure it in place with backfilled soil.

6 Place the waterfall stones in position (see page 38), working from the pond edge upwards to the header pool. Install the pump and delivery hose (see pages 37–8). Test the waterfall, and make any necessary adjustments.

7 Arrange the rocks on the banks of the pond. The stones should be staggered and variable in height. Build as much interest and detail as you can into the line of stones. Take great care when placing stones on the liner. Use offcuts as additional protection between the base of the stones and the liner.

8 For the damp bog areas, build a retaining wall up from the base of the pond, using concrete blocks set on a concrete base, 10cm (4in) deep. Protect the liner with plyboard while you work. Build the block wall up to within 30cm (1ft) of the water level, then backfill with soil. Cover the top of the wall, to just above water level, with a row of rough walling stones set with their bases in mortar into which a waterproofing additive has been mixed (see page 23). There

BOG AREA

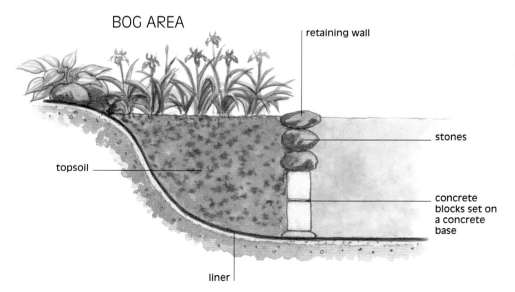

retaining wall

stones

topsoil

concrete
blocks set on
a concrete
base

liner

蓬萊島

should be no mortar between the stones, however, so that water can make its way into the bed. Bring the topsoil behind the wall up to the rear of the stones. Plant up the iris bed, using bold swathes of the same variety or colour. Initially, space the plants about 45cm (18in) apart.

9 Build up the island from the pond base by creating a retaining wall in the same way as above (see also page 36). Where the bridge is to meet the island, create the base using brick or flat stone. The base for the bridge should be the same width as the bridge itself. Backfill the island with topsoil, and install the stone bridge (see page 41).

10 Complete the shaping of the ground. The area in front of the pond should be level, and the area

behind it sculpted into a series of rolling mounds using subsoil and topsoil as before (see step 4). Grass over the mounds with seed or turf.

11 Cover the bank on the far side which gently slopes into the pond with cobbles and gravel, to resemble a pebble beach. Grade the stones in size, to add interest. Make sure that the liner finishes above the final water level. At the base of the slope place a row of concrete blocks laid on their side to support the cobbles. Lay a bed of mortar 5cm (2in) deep over the liner. Smooth the surface, working the mortar into any gaps between the stones lining the sides of the pond. While the mortar is still soft, press cobbles or gravel into the mortar bed; bringing the cobble beach up onto the shore.

12 Build up pedestals for the stepping stones from the pond base, either in block or stone (see pages 36–7).

13 Create the sitting area with paving slabs (see page 77) or timber decking (see pages 46–7). Make a simple screen of split bamboo canes, interspersed with vertical timber boards (see page 77), and place it behind the sitting area.

14 Place the low, flat stone on the beach and put the lantern on top of it. Plant around the edge of the pond, the waterfall and the island. Vary the heights of the planting, using drifts and tighter blocks of similar plants to give rhythm and accents to the scenery.

15 Fill the pond up to the desired water level. If wished, install garden lighting (see pages 54–5).

Above A waterfall can have a distinct mood which will influence the feeling of the viewer to the garden in general.

SIMPLE ARBOUR

The Waiting Arbour, or *Machiai*, is usually part of a Tea Garden. It takes many different forms, from a simple roofed shelter with portable seating to an elaborately constructed summer house or pavilion. In Japan, there is a highly developed and sophisticated craft of woodworking, as seen in their temples and Tea Houses.

Although not always practicable or attainable for most of us, such high standards can inspire us to modest creative efforts. In this project, we make a Machiai *as an addition to the garden setting. It does not have to be in keeping with the rest of the garden, but its position is important. It is usually elevated, to give fine views across the garden. The arbour should be a place to which you are tempted to retire with a cup of tea or a book. The path that leads the visitor to the arbour should provide some glimpses into the main garden, but not allow a full view over the garden – this should be enjoyed only from the seat of the arbour itself. The arbour should not be sited in splendid isolation, either; it should have enough planting of trees and shrubs around it to allow the structure to 'sit into the landscape'.*

Shopping list

Four rough-sawn or uncut timber
   posts, 10 x 10cm (4 x 4in),
   approximately 2.75m (9ft) long
Timbers for cross-members, as
   required
Concrete (see page 22), as
   required
Timber floorboards, at least
   2.5cm (1in) thick
Nails and screws
Exterior-grade plyboard for sides
   and roof
Plastic sheeting for roof
Timber shingles or thatching
   material (see pages 85–6)
Bamboo poles
Thin bamboo canes for detailing
Timbers for bench seat
Large, flat-topped stone
Stepping stones (optional)

Tools & equipment

Spade
Wooden site pegs
String line
Spirit level
Tape measure
Wood saw and chisel
Portable workbench
Stepladder
Hammer
Screwdriver
Power drill and bits

1 Draw a scaled plan of the arbour (including the front, side and rear elevations, a floor plan, and the roof structure) on paper, to allow you to calculate the measurements and the dimensions of the timbers required. Do not worry about the details of the finishing, as you will be able to add these once the main structure is standing. Think about the orientation of the arbour in relation to the movement of the sun: it is best to have the light coming from behind, especially in the evening, or from one side. You also need to decide whether or not to have a floor. The advantage of creating a raised floor to the arbour is twofold: raising the structure off the ground will help keep it dry,

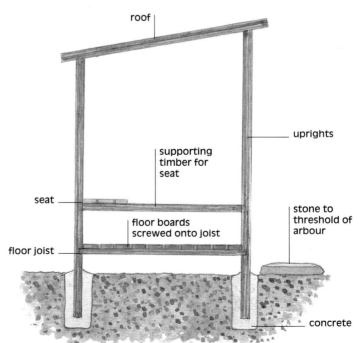

roof

uprights

supporting timber for seat

seat

floor boards screwed onto joist

floor joist

stone to threshold of arbour

concrete

Above The waiting arbour is a place to rest in the garden. Site it with a good view across the garden scenery.

and so increase its longevity; also, stepping up into the arbour, rather than simply walking into it at ground level, gives the visitor a positive sense of entering the arbour. In this example, there is a raised floor. At the planning stage, decide whether the floorboards are to run along the line of sight when seated, or at right angles to the viewer. When laid along the line of sight, the line of the boards naturally leads the eye out towards the garden scenery. The entrance path to the arbour should not be directly in the front, but offset to one side.

2   Clear the area for the arbour, allowing for a 'platform' approximately 5cm (2in) wider than the structure. Ensure that the ground is level, firm and compact underfoot. Mark the outline of the structure with pegs and string line. Make sure the layout is square by measuring the diagonals – they should be equal. At this stage, stand at the point where the seat will be and check that you are able to see well out into the garden; make any necessary adjustments to the layout.

3   Off site, cut the timbers for the uprights, calculating for 60cm (2ft) to be concreted into the ground, 15cm (6in) from ground level to the raised floor, and 2m (7ft) from floor to roof beams. Also prepare the timber frames for supporting both the floor and the roof, using simple half-lap joints. The cross members need to be jointed where they will meet one another,

Left When approaching a seat, prevent the viewer from seeing the view to be had from the seating position itself. This can be done by planning the line of approach, combined with screening plants.

and joints are also required where the floor joists and roof beams will be attached to the uprights. Calculate meticulously where each joint is required before starting work. When they are ready, fit the structural frame together.

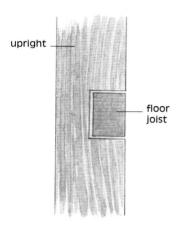

upright

floor joist

4 Take the framework to the site, and check that the height of the posts above ground is correct, that they are square to one another, and that the joints are all in the correct positions. Then set the uprights in concrete (see page 23) to a depth of 60cm (2ft). Do not level the concrete, but angle it up slightly towards the post; there will then be no possibility of water lying directly next to the timber and rotting the post.

5 The next stage is to fit the floor. Lay the boards across the supporting timber frame, leaving a slight gap between them to allow for any swelling of the timbers. Nail or preferably screw the boards to the supporting timbers.

6 Create the roof by screwing the plyboard sheeting to the frame. The eaves should extend beyond the front and sides of the base of the structure by at least 30cm (1ft). Nail or screw a plastic sheet

on top of the plyboard to keep the structure waterproof. Then cover the roof with wooden shingles or thatching material (see pages 85–6).

7 Cut and fit the plyboard to the back and sides of the arbour. When it is in place, cut a circular or oval opening as a window in one or both side panels. Consider the height of a person sitting on the bench seat when deciding where the opening should be. Any window should allow an interesting view out into the garden – if there is not a particularly good view in both directions, then you can create just one opening. You could also fit a series of thin bamboo canes across the opening, by nailing or screwing them at each side, to add further interest.

8 To make the seat, first attach a supporting timber to each side of the arbour, and another to the back, remembering that a comfortable height for a seat is about 45cm (18in) off the floor. The seat itself can be made with the same kind of boards that were used for the floor. Run the boards for the seat from side to side, and make it at least 45cm (18in) wide. For an interesting detail, fix a split bamboo strip between a couple of the boards, with the outside of the bamboo uppermost. For this

purpose, choose a cane that is long enough to extend right across the seat, fitting it so that its surface is flush with the boards.

9 Add some detailing to the interior of the arbour. For example, you could cover the underside of the roof with split-bamboo strips, fitted tight up to one another to give the impression that the roof structure is more complex than it actually is. If you added thin bamboo canes to the window opening (see step 7), you could now also wind some wisteria tendrils around the bamboo canes, if there is a plant already growing nearby or you are able to plant one below the window specially for the purpose. Choose shoots that are beginning to become woody, but are still pliable enough to wind in open turns around the canes without splitting.

10 Put in position the large flat-topped stone as the entry point to the arbour. In Japanese, this stone is known as the *kutsunugi ishi* (or 'shoe leaving stone'), as it is the custom to remove your shoes before entering a building. This stone should be set at a height about halfway between the levels of the ground and the floor. If desired, add some stepping stones (see pages 44–5) that will lead the visitor to the entry point.

PLAN VIEW OF FLOOR

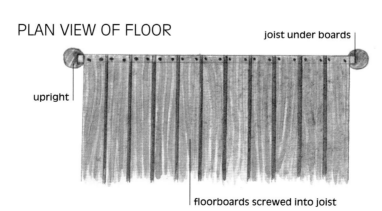

joist under boards

upright

floorboards screwed into joist

WINDING STREAM

The *Yarimizu*, or Winding Stream, has been a feature of Japanese gardens for centuries. It is a slow-moving, shallow stream, often quite narrow, making its sinuous way across an open garden. The land inside a river bend was thought to be particularly auspicious, so the winding stream of the courtyard was probably designed to create the beneficial 'inside bend' view from the rooms that overlooked the garden.

The stream suits a site where there is a gentle cross fall to the garden, and there is generous width to work with. The stream could be brought down toward the house and crossed by the bridge to reach the remainder of the garden beyond. The stream can terminate in a pond or an underground tank. If using a pond, remember that the stream will reduce the water level in the pond to a degree, so the pond should be large enough to hold plenty of water. In our project, we are using a tank, and screening it with an iris planting. Butyl pond liners can be heat-welded to order, and you will need to arrange this before you start. The extra piece allows for a generous iris garden.

Shopping list

Crushed hardcore, as required

Sand, as required

Container, or concrete manhole rings, for reservoir tank

Mortar (see page 23), as required

Mortar waterproofing additive

Water pump capable of delivering 1,130–1,360 litres (250–300 gallons) per hour (see page 37)

Delivery hose

Butyl pond liner, 1.8m (6ft) in width, with another piece 3.5 x 5.5m (12 x 18ft) welded to the end (see page 37)

Low, rounded stone water basin

Selected pieces of rockery stone

Flat-topped cobbles

Concrete (see page 22), as required

Coarse gravel (see page 30)

Cobbles of varying sizes

Thin strips of walling stone

Grass seed or turf, as required

Timber plank, 20 x 5cm (8 x 2in), at least 1.8m (6ft) long

Stepping stones

Section of fencing (see pages 62–3)

Plants such as irises, *Primula florindae*, *Hosta elegans*, *Rodgersia pinnata* 'Superba', *Schizostylis coccinea*, ferns such as *Osmunda regalis*, specimen trees or shrubs and low mounded evergreens

Tools & equipment

Wooden site pegs

String line

Spade

Spirit level

Vibrating plate compactor (from a hire shop)

Wheelbarrow

Pointing trowel

Sharp knife

Rake

Left This winding watercourse is modelled after a rocky upland stream, blending different sizes of stone.

1 Several aspects of this project need particular care at the planning stage. The flow of water must be correct; it should not flow like a torrent, but lazily make its way downstream. In the lower part of the feature the water can be dammed with low rills to cause a pool of slow water. In the upper part of the stream, the water should be very shallow. The bed of the stream must be quite level in cross-section. The detailing of the stream bed is important, as it will have a direct bearing on the patterns of water flow. Vary the texture of the bed where the depth of water is most shallow. The deeper, slower sections can be 5–8cm (2–3in) deep. The stream should widen as it reaches the lower sections, varying from 60cm (2ft) wide to perhaps 90cm (3ft). Roughly calculate the capacity of

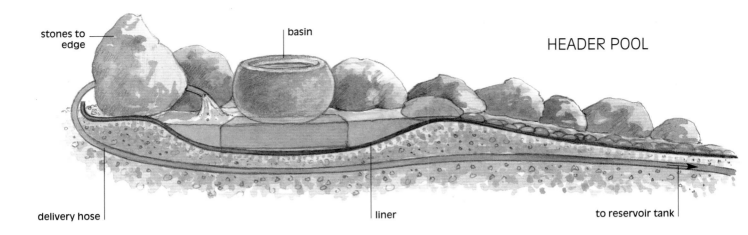

stones to edge

basin

HEADER POOL

delivery hose

liner

to reservoir tank

the streamcourse to hold water, by multiplying the length of the stream by the average depth, say 5cm (2in). The reservoir tank will have to store that capacity of water, even though some water will be retained in the stream at all times. To work best, this project requires a site with a slight cross fall to it, and is best located in an open area. It is possible to cut such a stream through an existing lawn, and retain some lawn running up to the stream edge.

2   Mark out and excavate the streamcourse (see page 37), allowing at least 30cm (1ft) extra on each side of the finished stream width. Keep the topsoil from the stream excavation for later use. Make sure that the bed is level in cross-section. Leave the occasional step in the lower section of the bed for the rills. Cover the base with hardcore and sand (see page 37), and compact it with a vibrating plate compactor.

Practicalities

As the stream will lose water through evaporation, fit a self-topping mechanism to the mains water supply. This will automatically top up the reservoir tank.

3   Dig out the hole for the reservoir tank at the end of the stream bed. The resulting large volume of soil is probably best taken off the site, as it will mainly be subsoil. If using a large container for the reservoir, place it in the hole. If using concrete manhole ring sections, place them one on top of the other, sealing the sections together with a pliable mortar (see page 23). Take great care when moving and assembling the sections, as they are extremely heavy. When all the rings are in place, render the inside of the tank with a layer of mortar with a waterproof additive mixed into it. When this is dry, add a second 'skin' of mortar. Install the pump in the tank (see page 37), and attach the delivery hose.

4   Dig out the areas for the iris garden near the end of the stream bed to a depth of 30cm (1ft), keeping the topsoil on one side. Place the liner along the streamcourse and over the bog garden area. Where the liner follows the bends in the stream, make sure that the folds you will need to make in the liner are neat and all follow one direction. Build the bog garden (see page 116).

5   For the header pool, place the water basin in a shallow pool at the

top of stream. Lead the delivery hose from the reservoir into the top of the header pool and disguise the end of it by covering it with stones. Make sure that the stones positioned around the perimeter of the header pool rise well above the water level, and that the liner is brought up well behind them.

6   Cover the streamcourse with a thin bed of concrete, pressing a coarse gravel into the wet mix as you work down. Take care to maintain the level of the stream bed as you work. Cover the stream bed with small cobbles.

7   Build the stone rills across the stream to create small dams. Either cement a row of flat-topped cobbles to the bed, ensuring that the tops are level, and discreetly point between the stones, trying not to allow any mortar to show. Or place one large flat stone across the stream to create a rill.

8   Place large, rounded cobbles at the outside of the bends of the stream in small groups. Using flat, thin strips of walling stone, create a very low wall along the edges of the lower section of the stream. Make sure the walls are above the finished water

CREATING RILLS

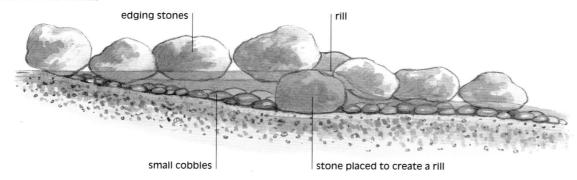

edging stones | rill

small cobbles | stone placed to create a rill

level. Fold the liner up the back of the low wall, and hold it in place with backfilled topsoil. Any turf removed earlier can be relaid right up to the back of the stones and walls.

9 Switch on the pump and test the water flow. Make adjustments until you are satisfied with the flow of water in the stream.

10 Create the planting mounds using the topsoil removed from the stream excavation. The shapes should be very subtle, with long, low rises and falls in the ground surfaces. Mould the ground levels around the stream so that they appear quite natural. The mounds will be mainly covered with grass to blend in with the surrounding lawn areas. Turfing or seeding can be carried out either now or later, as desired.

11 Lay the plank across the stream, supporting it on either side with pieces of rockery stone. Make sure the bridge is at least twice as long as the stream is wide. The bridge can either be straight or at an angle. If straight, make sure it is offset from the angle of approach. Do not fit a handrail, as this will spoil the simple lines of the bridge.

12 Lay the stepping-stone path (see pages 44–5).

13 Erect the fencework over the iris beds (see page 63). Continue the fence well beyond the reservoir tank and iris garden in both directions. The fence need be no more than 1.2m (4ft) high. Where any vertical bamboo poles cross the stream, support the end of each pole on a rock projecting from the stream bed to prevent them getting damp.

14 Plant the bog garden with irises or other suitable plants (see page 39). Planting for the mounds should be sparse and concentrated into a few areas. In these areas, arrange a sculpted specimen shrub or small tree, such as a pine, as a focal point. Around this, add a few groups of low clipped mounds of evergreen foliage as if you were placing large rocks. Plant around the reservoir tank with evergreen shrubs, and trim them into large billowing masses as they grow.

Left The wooden bridge in this project is a simple timber plank but it must be fixed securely.

Three Weekend Projects

CLASSICAL HILL GARDEN

The Hill Garden, or *Tsukiyama niwa*, is one of the three classical styles of garden in Japan. The others are the Flat Garden and the Tea Garden (see page 134). The Hill Garden may be large or small, and is usually centred around an expanse of water, or gravel 'Sea' in the case of a 'dry landscape' interpretation such as the example shown here.

The body of water or gravel is framed by a series of hills, arranged with great care, and usually has an island, which may be connected to the shoreline by bridges. There are five principal hills in our example. The Near Hill is the tallest, and creates a partial screen concealing the view as the visitor approaches. The Distant Hill is sited roughly in the centre of the composition, and is approximately two-thirds the height of the Near Hill. The Far Distance Hill is about a third lower again than the Distant Hill, and part of this hill is concealed by the Distant Hill. The Companion Hill is on the left, and about the same height as the Far Distance Hill. The Side Hill is on the right, and lower than the Companion Hill.

Tools & equipment

Wooden site pegs
String line
Spade
Wheelbarrow
Mini-digger for larger schemes
    (from a hire shop)
Stone-moving equipment (see
    pages 24–5)
Gravel rake (see pages 48–9)

Shopping list

Topsoil, as required

Selected rockery stones of various shapes

Rounded timber posts

Concrete (see page 22), as required

Rounded cobbles in various sizes

Large, flat-topped rock

One or two stone slabs or wide, heavy timbers for bridges

Gravel (see page 30) or stepping stones for paths

Timber decking (see pages 46–7) or paving stones

Two stone lanterns (see pages 52–3), one larger than the other

Evergreen shrubs such as azaleas

Ornamental grasses

Geotextile sheeting (see page 30)

Small-diameter (8–10mm/¼–½in) light-coloured gravel, as required

1 Carry out a survey of the area, making a note of existing features that can be retained. Note carefully what there is beyond the garden's boundaries which may be visually incorporated into the garden scheme, and also any features which will require screening from view. Observe the manner in which the garden is approached, and from where it is best seen. Although the garden may be a self-contained creation, it must always link to and relate to the wider landscape.

2 Draw a detailed plan. When planning the outline of the gravel sea, make sure that the shoreline is of interest, with bays and inlets, and check that not all of the area can be seen from any one position in the garden. Where parts of the landscape disappear out of sight, it leads the eye to believe that the

area is larger than it actually is. The placing of paths through the area is important, because they form the principal route through the garden and represent the eyeline of the viewer. Avoid placing the paths so that all the line of the path is visible; it is much better to have the path appearing and disappearing from view. Ensure that all the various elements of the composition link to each another.

3 Mark out the area for the gravel 'sea' using wooden pegs and string. Dig out and level the area, lowering its surface by about 10cm (4in) to accommodate the covering of gravel.

4 Use all the excavated soil to create the hill shapes, according to the plan. If there is not enough, import some fresh topsoil. For the core of the hill shapes, use the heavier

subsoil, and cover it with a layer of better-quality topsoil to form the final shape.

5 Put the rock arrangements in place. Avoid overcrowding the scenery with too many rocks, as this will distract the eye. The main rock arrangement is near the Distant Hill, and consists of a rock group suggestive of a waterfall. A flat-topped waterfall face stone, flanked either side by low upright stones, is the minimum requirement. Above this, place a tall upright stone – this is the Principal stone of the whole garden, and each of the other stones should relate in its position and attitude to this unifying stone. The stones arranged in the foreground of the composition can be larger and taller than the stones placed in the rear of the garden. The distant stones should

Above The garden at the Adachi Museum, near Okayana, uses striking rock arrangements combined with ground shapes to evoke landscape on a grand scale.

PLAN VIEW

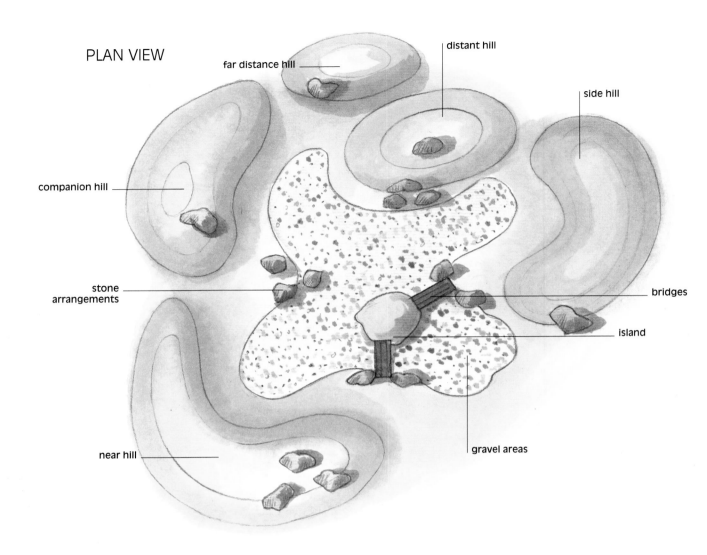

far distance hill

distant hill

side hill

companion hill

stone arrangements

bridges

island

near hill

gravel areas

also be smooth and rounded in outline, whereas the stones in the foreground can be more rugged and textured.

6 Add detail to the shoreline of the gravel sea. Place stones so as to suggest cliff faces rising vertically from the 'water'. In other areas, use rounded posts, concreted into place, to retain the bank. Add a promontory of rocks running out into the 'water', and create a beach section with rounded cobbles in varying sizes (see pages 116–17). Place on the near shoreline one large, flat-topped rock; this is the viewing stone.

7 Build the island with soil, edged with stone, towards the near side of the pond as it is approached – this allows for a relatively large area of gravel behind it to give the impression of space. Add closely set rocks of a rugged nature to the shoreline of the island. Create two simple bridges using timber or flat stones (see page 41). One bridge runs from the near shore across to the island, and the other leads from the island back to the shore in the middle distance. Do not align the bridges in a straight line, but instead set them at an angle to one another. Position the anchor stones for each bridge (see pages 40–41).

8 In larger garden layouts, surface the paths with gravel, and in smaller ones use stepping stones (see pages 44–5). A section of path should lead to the viewing stone.

9 The garden is to be seen primarily from a small viewing area in the front. This should be sited slightly away from the path route, perhaps with a few stepping stones leading to it. Use timber decking (see pages 46–7) or lay paving slabs (see page 77) to create the platform.

10 Carefully position the stone lanterns. Place the taller one at

the front of the scenery, and the smaller, lower one in the background, to enhance the feeling of distance.

11 Plant up the garden, still following the principle of tall elements at the front and smaller ones at the back. You can further enhance this by placing plants with larger leaves in the foreground and smaller-leaved plants in the background. At key locations, put some shaped plants, and add some low, clipped mounds to represent plants seen from afar. Do not overplant the garden; arrange the planting into groups based on the locations of the rocks, leaving open spaces between the groups.

12 Finally create the gravel sea. First lay geotextile sheeting over the area. Spread the gravel out until the surface is perfectly level, then rake it into patterns suggestive of flowing or moving water. If you have a large gravel area, consider raking the gravel in the foreground and brushing smooth the gravel in the background, to emphasize the illusion of distance.

Below Shaping the ground is one of the first tasks in creating a garden. It may be possible to move existing earth, or it may need importing to create raised areas.

SPRING AND AUTUMN GARDEN

The spring and autumn seasons are the times when a Japanese garden comes to a climax in terms of colour. During the summer, the garden reverts to an emphasis on the arrangement of forms, and colour is a limited palette of greens of many different shades, in contrast to most Western gardens which tend to bloom in the summer months.

In this project, we are looking in particular at the planting of the garden to emphasize spring and autumn. One way to achieve this is to create different zones within the garden, each placing emphasis on a group of plants for a different season. In our example, there are six zones: two each for spring and autumn, one for summer, and one neutral. The neutral zone represents 'empty space' in the composition, and is used for the lawn. The spring zones should be planted with cherry and plum trees (Prunus spp.), for their blossom, surrounded by other spring-flowering plants (see page 142), including evergreen azaleas. Use Japanese maples (Acer spp.) and other shrubs with autumn tints (see page 142) for the autumn areas. Make a selection of a small number of species which thrive in your area and plant them in numbers through the garden for maximum effect.

SPRING GARDEN

Shopping list

Timber decking (see pages 46–7)

Nails or screws

Bench seat

Square trellis panels, as required

Bamboo canes

Black twine

Summer-flowering climber such as jasmine

Selection of rockery stones

Stepping stones

Large, flat stone

Rounded logs, 8cm (3in) in diameter, as required

Concrete (see page 22), as required

Dark-coloured wood stain

Geotextile sheeting (see page 30)

Cobbles

Two pieces of timber or two long, flat stone slabs for bridges

Low stone water basin arrangement (see page 64)

Short section of 'sleeve' fencing (see page 28)

Organic matter such as leafmould or garden compost

Plants for seasonal displays (see page 142)

Evergreen ferns

Gravel (see page 30), as required

Fine-grained mulch

Tools & equipment

Wooden site pegs

String line

Spade

Wheelbarrow

Wood saw

Hammer or screwdriver

Spirit level

Stone-moving equipment (see pages 24–5)

Mallet

Paintbrush

Sharp knife

Gravel rake (see pages 48–9)

PLANTING ZONES

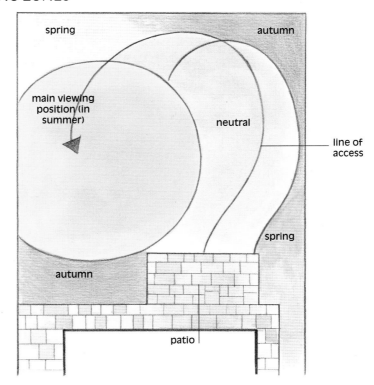

1 Make a survey of the area. Loosely sketch over it a pattern of lines that divides the garden into a series of zones, and then designate a season to each. Keep the design very fluid at first, and try to create a sense of movement with the layout. The summer zone, for example, should be the best place to sit on long, warm days; so site the decking there, and make it the final destination of a walk around the garden. With this basic pattern underlying the design, sketch in the ground shapes, main features, paths, lawn area, and so on. The decking should be large enough to accommodate a bench seat. In this sort of garden, the rock arrangements are confined to certain key features. Most of the season zones should have a rock arrangement – this need be no more than three stones, or perhaps even a single fine stone. The positioning of the rocks will give a structure to each area. Once you have the main structure of the various garden zones in place, gradually work on the development of the planting. Fine-tune all the elements of the sketch plan until you are satisfied.

2 Mark out the zones of the site with pegs and string line. Clear and level the area for the gravel to a depth of 12cm (5in).

3 Using the excavated topsoil (you may have to supplement this with fresh topsoil), create the gentle mounds, including the headland and the island in the gravel, ensuring that they are not all the same height.

4 Assemble the timber decking (see pages 46–7) to a height of 30cm (1ft) above the finished level of the gravel. Bring in and position the bench seat.

Above Autumn colours give the garden the impression of bursting into flame. The strong colours give an intensity of excitement to the eye.

5 Make a simple and inexpensive screen from square trellis panels to which a series of split bamboo canes have been attached vertically and tied with black twine. Erect this behind the decking. Plant a climber to grow up and through the trellis.

6 Place the rockery stones in position, so as to create a rocky shoreline around the headland and the island. When placing these stones, try to position them so as to give them a rugged look. Add a small group of particularly interesting stones to the front of the gravel area, to represent individual rocky islands.

7 Create the stepping-stone path (see pages 44–5), setting the stones 5cm (2in) above ground level. To add interest, break up the sequence with a short section of path in which the stones are grouped tightly together. Where the path leads to the edge of the gravel area, set the large, flat stone as a viewing stone.

8 Add the line of low, rounded logs to retain the gravel. Dig out a trench 30cm (1ft) deep, and fix the logs upright in a bed of concrete (see page 22), 15cm (6in) deep, to hold them at the base. The tops of the logs should be about 10cm (4in) above the finished level of the gravel. Where the logs abut the lawn, make sure the logs and the lawn are at the same level. Stain the logs with a dark stain.

9 Cover the whole of the gravel area with geotextile sheeting, and trim it to size. Lay the cobbles to create the 'beach' on top of the geo-textile sheeting.

10 Put the long, flat bridge stones or timbers in place to create the two bridges (see page 41).

11 Create a water basin arrangement by the patio as described on pages 64–5, allowing space at the back for some evergreen shrubs that can be grown on to about 1.5m (5ft) in height. Use the 'sleeve' fencing (see page 28) to separate the water basin area from the rest of the garden. You could fill the

basin with fresh water by hand, or alternatively pump water into the basin through a bamboo spout (see pages 64–5).

12 Prepare all the planting areas thoroughly by double digging the soil (see page 75), removing all stones and other debris. Improve the soil by introducing plenty of organic matter. Time taken preparing the soil properly before planting will pay dividends in good plant establishment and healthy plants. Check that the planting areas are not subject to drainage problems (see page 155).

13 Plant the structural plants such as trees and shrubs intended to grow into large specimens. Then add in the 'understorey' planting, using the rock groupings to guide you. Group the plants, and do not be afraid to leave gaps between the groups. Add detailed planting in places such as between the stones of the rocky shoreline, using plants such as evergreen ferns.

14 Spread and level the gravel over the geotextile sheeting. Rake it into a pattern, if desired (see pages 48–9). Tidy all parts of the garden. Mulch areas of bare soil.

AUTUMN GARDEN

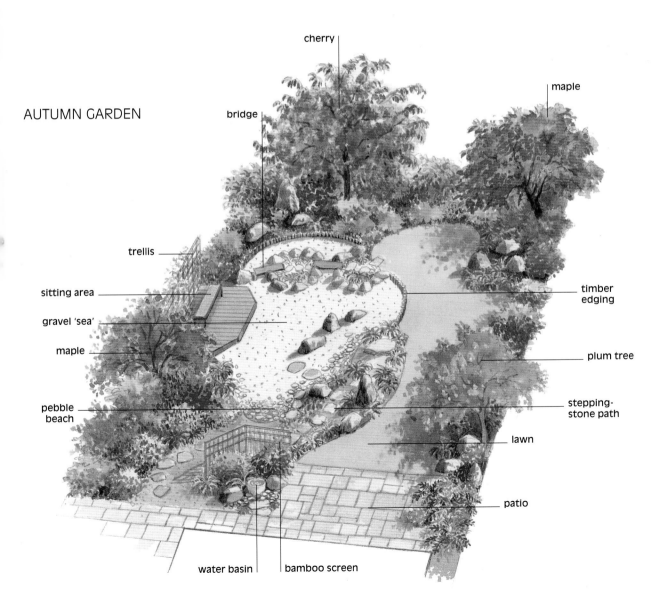

cherry

maple

bridge

trellis

sitting area

gravel 'sea'

maple

pebble beach

timber edging

plum tree

stepping-stone path

lawn

patio

water basin | bamboo screen

TEA GARDEN

The Tea House, where the Tea Ceremony takes place (see page 9), is a simple building, often approached via some stepping stones and a water basin. There are few rules regarding the exact configuration of a traditional Japanese Tea Garden, though one important principle stands out – the garden should be as unostentatious as possible.

A Tea Garden should be self-contained. It is often divided into two parts, the Inner and Outer Gardens, separated by the Middle Gate, here a bamboo fence. As the garden is essentially a pathway, it can be fitted into any configuration of space. In our main example, we are using a long, narrow site. The entry point is important, and therefore marked by a simple, roofed gate. The water basin is close to the gate, reached by a short side path. Keep the Outer and Inner Gardens different in mood, for example by planting one sparsely and the other densely. The line of the path should meander to its destination so that guests, while walking calmly along the path, gradually leave behind the cares of the everyday world, enabling them to enter the Tea House with a fresh, unencumbered mind and heart.

Tools & equipment

Spade
Wooden site pegs
String line
Spirit level
Stone-moving equipment (see
    pages 24–5)
Pointing trowel
Wood saw
Hammer
Rake
Brush

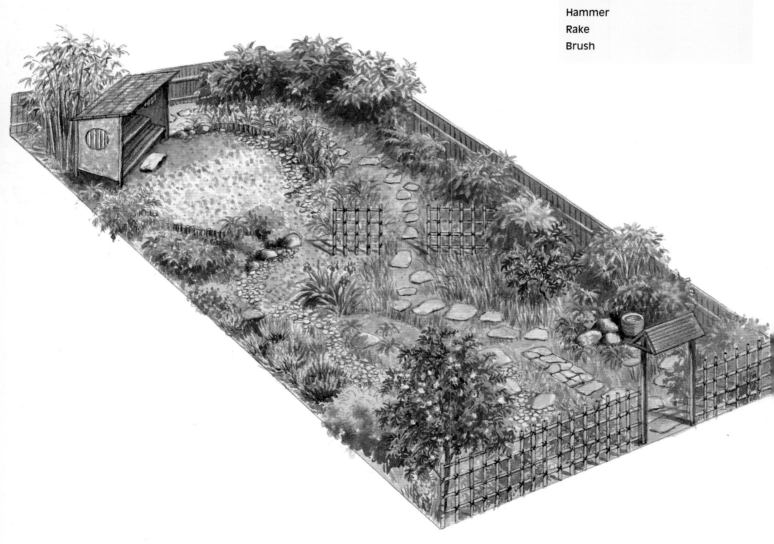

Shopping list

Stone water basin arrangement (see pages 64–5)

Evergreen shrubs, such as *Aucuba japonica*

Stepping stones

Hardcore, as required

Mortar (see page 23), as required

Entry gate (see pages 84–7)

Rough stone slabs

Concrete (see page 22), as required

Sections of fencing (see pages 28–9)

Bamboo fence (see pages 62–3)

Simple Waiting Arbour or *Machiai* (see page 118–21)

Selection of rockery stones

Geotextile sheeting (see page 30)

Rounded logs, 8cm (3in) in diameter, 30cm (1ft) long

Rounded cobbles in various sizes

Gravel (see page 30)

Trees such as *Crataegus monogyna* and *Sorbus matsumurana*

Evergreen shrubs such as azaleas and bamboos

Wild flowers

1 Make a survey of the area, and then draw up a sketch plan incorporating all the desired elements, and retaining any suitable existing plants. Generally, the ground levels can be utilized as they are found. If there are rises and falls on the site, plan to incorporate these as part of the layout. Make sure when siting the Entry Gate that it does not face directly on to a view of the *Machiai*. The style of the boundary fence can vary from a simple *Yotsume gaki*, the see-through 'four-eyed fence', to a more solid type of fencework (see pages 28–9). The Tea Garden should be fairly isolated from the remainder of the garden. Fencing within the Tea Garden

should be low and open in look; again, *Yotsume gaki* is commonly used. The thickness of the canes should be no more than 5cm (2in), with the vertical canes set well apart so that the fencework has a light feel about it. The finished fence should not be any higher than 90cm (3ft). The Middle Gate, which leads from the Outer Garden to the Inner Garden, should be a simple construction of bamboo, rustic poles or even branches.

2 Clear the site. With wooden pegs and string line, mark out the relative positions of the Entry Gate, the Middle Gate, the *Machiai*, and the gravel 'pool' with its 'stream' meandering away from it.

3 Excavate the area for the gravel 'pool', and use the soil that you have removed to mound up the area on the left of the Entry Gate. Level out the area where the *Machiai* is to stand.

Above The Tea Garden should be of the utmost simplicity and quietness in mood.

4 Create a water basin arrangement (as described on pages 64–5). Position it so that it is framed by the upright posts of the Entry Gate as the visitor approaches the garden. Plant a group of evergreen shrubs such as *Aucuba japonica* densely behind the water basin so that they will screen the view of the rest of the garden. The basin should be sited on one side of the main stepping-stone path and reached by another couple of stepping stones.

Below The Tea Garden uses very little colour and avoids dramatic arrangements.

5 Lay the stepping stones for the path (see pages 44–5) so that they sit 5–8cm (2–3in) above ground level. For the solid 'pavement'

PAVEMENT PATH

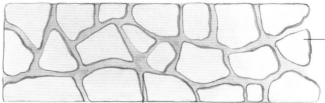

pieces of stone laid on a compacted hardcore base

the stones should 'fit' together, do not butt two pointed parts of the stone

sections of the path, first lay a compacted hardcore base, 10–15cm (4–6in) deep, and then fit pieces of stone together on top of it, in the same way as for crazy paving. Point with mortar between the stones, leaving the pointing slightly recessed below the level of the surface of the stones.

6 Build and then erect the Entry Gate (see pages 84–7). Next make a small paved area at the base of the gateway, constructed from rough stone slabs laid on a concrete base, 10cm (4in) deep. Do not point with mortar between the stone slabs, but instead fill the narrow gaps with sieved garden soil.

ALTERNATIVE PLAN FOR A SQUARE GARDEN

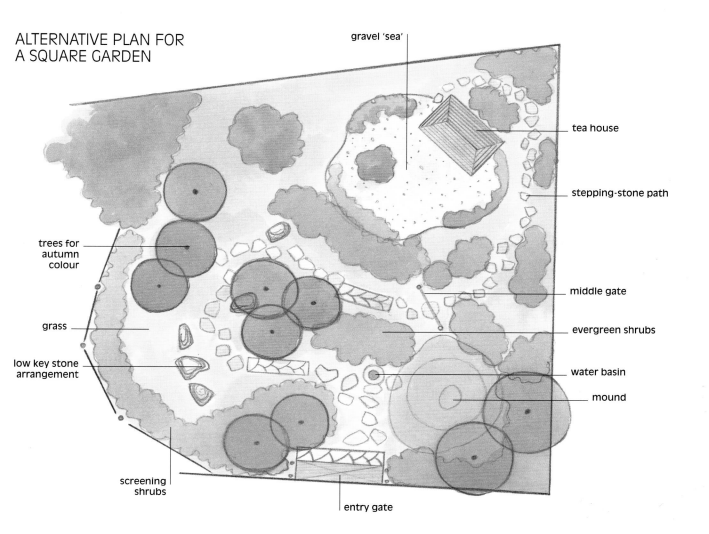

gravel 'sea'

tea house

stepping-stone path

trees for autumn colour

middle gate

grass

evergreen shrubs

low key stone arrangement

water basin

mound

screening shrubs

entry gate

7 Erect both the boundary fencing and the fencing that will separate the Outer and Inner Gardens (see pages 62–3).

8 Build and erect the *Machiai*, as described on pages 118–121, with the entrance to it positioned on one side. Set the base of the pavilion so that it overhangs the gravel area in front of it by about 60cm (2ft). The front support posts of the building should rest on flat-topped rockery stones that are set in the gravel.

9 Line the area for the gravel 'pool' and 'stream' with geotextile sheeting. Edge the area with a line of round logs set vertically (see page 132) and cobble beach

areas (see page 117). The streamcourse should become narrower as it winds towards its 'source'. Cover the stream bed with cobbles of varying sizes, and spread the gravel over the area of the 'pool'.

10 Place the rockery stones in the Outer Garden only. They can be positioned so that they can be seen from within the Inner Garden, but there should not be any of the stones actually in the latter area. The stones you select should be simple in their shape and texture, and arranged in a loose, open manner – do not create regimented groupings. The stones positioned at the 'source' of the stream should not be large.

11 Plant the Outer Garden with trees and shrubs. The boundaries of the garden should be thickly planted, to make the garden area seem enclosed. Arrange the planting in small groups with plenty of space around them. Bamboos are good for this purpose. Cover the ground with long grass and suitable wild flowers. This will require cutting only once or twice a year. Plant the Inner Garden much more sparsely, to create a striking contrast.

12 Sweep the surface of the gravel pool flat and level with a brush.

13 If your garden is more square than long and narrow in shape, you could follow the alternative plan illustrated above.

Plants are the 'flesh on the bones' of any garden. This chapter explores the best kinds of plants to use when creating a Japanese-style garden, and how to develop them as features within a composition. With certain plants this can be achieved by regular pruning and training and these techniques are covered here.

PLANTS AND PRUNING

Plants and Pruning

SUITABLE PLANTS

There is a wide range of plants suitable for use in the Japanese garden. You only have to think of the number of plants native to Japan to appreciate that the palette is indeed extensive. Having said that, a visit to contemporary gardens in Japan reveals that, of this large potential pool of plants, the number of species used is relatively small.

There are many gardens that feature azaleas as the sole plant type. It is not that the Japanese have disregarded the wealth of native plant material for their gardens, but rather that they have exercised great restraint.

The Western garden has tended toward the opposite effect, and to some degree the measure of a gardener's skill is related to the number and rarity of plants he or she is able to grow in the garden space. The result of the travels and explorations of the great plant-hunters of the past and present means that there is a vast selection of plants available to the gardener today. The problem is not one so much of availability as one of suitability to the specific climatic conditions prevailing in the garden.

Plants in Japanese garden design

The plants traditionally used in the gardens of Japan were ones that were readily available to the gardeners. They collected plants from the surrounding mountains and valleys in order to stock their gardens. Advice offered in the old garden texts is to put in those plants that are most suited to the kind of garden being created – meaning that you should use mountain plants for the 'mountain' areas, and plants of the plains and valleys for those types of areas within the garden. A misconception that has arisen among garden creators in the West when building a Japanese garden is that all the plants for the garden need to be of Japanese origin. It is much more important that the plant selection for the garden reflects those plants that can be used successfully in the locality of the garden. It would be unwise to limit yourself to an artificially restricted list of plants that might not be suitable for your growing conditions. Many plants of Japanese origin, such as azaleas, require acidic soil, but this is not suitable for all locations. Therefore, you need to understand the role plants can play in the garden, and then seek out those that are most suitable for your particular area.

When designing a Japanese garden, think of the plants as textures and shapes to work with. You are not concerned with establishing borders of successive waves of colour, but rather with brief, sharp, seasonal bursts of colour, after which the garden falls back to a restful state. The two seasons to emphasize are spring, celebrating the renewal of the year, and autumn, noting the coming of winter. Bear in mind that, in the context of the overall design, planting has a subservient role to play to the patterns of stone arrangements. Where the stones are considered to constitute the 'skeleton of the garden', the planting is seen as being the 'flesh on the bones' of the main garden structures. This arises not out of a disregard for the role of plants, but because of the importance of shape, form and texture within the design. The planting fulfils a role which is more to do with linking passages of the garden together, softening and screening. It is, in fact, quite a balanced view of the garden, where all the various elements are seen in terms of the particular roles and functions they are intended to perform.

Special plants

In Japanese tradition, there are three plants in particular which are highly revered. Frequently referred to as the 'Three Friends', these are the plum (*Prunus mume*), pine (*Pinus thunbergii*) and bamboo (*Phyllostachys* spp.). They are respected and admired for the qualities they exhibit. The plum flowers in the very early part of the spring when the weather can still be very cold, the pine has long been associated with tenacity and longevity, and the bamboo is admired for its resilience and strength.

Below Bamboos are best grown with clear stems, this allows the eye to see the scenery through the strong vertical lines.

Above Cherry blossom is highly evocative of Japan. The single-flowered varieties are preferred for the delicacy of the light in the foliage.

Left Pines are commonly used in Japanese gardens. The trees are tended by hand several times a year in order to thin the needles and shape the branches.

Spring and autumn colour

In spring, when the cherry blossom is reaching its brief peak, millions of Japanese people take themselves out to the parks and other gardens to view it. Businesses even take short holidays, and the staff decamp to celebrate and enjoy a day of feasting and merriment under the blossom. The flowering of the cherry trees is a national event. The autumn sees a similar, though slightly more restrained, exodus to those places where the maple trees (*Acer* spp.) can be seen in wonderfully vivid colours. Every year in the Kyoto area there are special seasonal openings of gardens to enable people to enjoy them when they are at their most resplendent. Despite this outbreak of seasonal fervour, however, the role of colour in the Japanese garden is quite different to that in the Western garden. Colour is perceived as being a transitory and fleeting element, and its use is concerned much more with creating a seasonal impact than a year-round effect.

There are also wild plants that are associated with the very early spring, known as the 'Seven Herbs of Spring'; they have been revered for hundreds of years in poetry. These are water parsley (*Oenanthe stolonifera*), white turnip (*Brassica campestris*), shepherd's purse (*Capsella bursa-pastoris*), chickweed (*Stellaria media*), cudweed (*Gnaphalium multiceps*), deadnettle (*Lamium amplexicaule*) and Japanese white radish (*Raphanus sativus*).

Where spring-flowering cherry trees are concerned, single-flowered varieties are preferred to double. *Prunus cerasifera* 'Pissardii' and *P. x subhirtella* 'Accolade' are cherry trees that are suitable for small gardens, though cherries do have the habit of developing roots near the ground surface, which can become a nuisance in later years as the trees age.

Likewise, there are plants that are notable because they are said to be evocative of autumn, known as the 'Seven Flowers of Autumn'. These are fringed pink (*Dianthus superbus*), bush clover (*Lespedeza bicolor*), ominaeshi (*Patrinia scabiosaefolia*), Japanese reed grass (*Miscanthus sinensis*), fujibakama (*Eupatorium stoechadosmum*), kudzu vine (*Pueraria thunbergiana*), and morning glory (*Ipomoea* spp.). For autumn colour in the smaller garden, the Japanese maples (*Acer* spp.) are perfect; they tend to be expensive to buy at specimen size, but if nurtured and fed will make good growth in a few years. There are many shrubs which will provide good autumn colour, such as *Fothergilla major*, which produces spectacular tints.

Evergreen plants

Of all the plants used in Japanese gardens, the overwhelming majority are evergreens. This is because the planting is used for creating shapes and mass in the garden design rather than colour. It also lends a sense of timelessness to the garden, which is an important consideration. The use of evergreen plants means the gardens are predominantly a blending of numerous shades of green – this partially explains why the gardens can give the impression of being so restful. Of all the colours in the spectrum, green is seen to be the most calming and soothing. The over-use of bright and strong colours can tire the viewer's eye, yet when colour appears in the garden against a backdrop of green the effect of that colour will be magnified in its intensity.

Fewer flowers in the garden can make a powerful impact on the viewer – as encapsulated in the old adage of 'less is more'. An interesting story concerns the 16th-century Tea Master Sen no Rikyu, who cultivated some morning glory. The Shogun Hideyoshi received word of the beauty of the flowers that Rikyu was growing, and determined to pay a visit to see the flowers for himself. When he arrived in the garden, there was not one flower to be seen; all had been carefully removed. To allay the supreme ruler's fury, Rikyu invited him into the Tea Room, where in the most prominent place was a single, perfect, morning glory flower.

Shape and texture

Planting provides shape and texture as well as colour. Colour is a transitory or fleeting moment in the life of the plant. The value of texture is that it may be used as a constant presence (in the case of evergreens) in the composition. Against this background, seasonal effects can be played off. Thinking in terms of texture means identifying useful plants that have certain characteristics and uses, such as:

1 plants that create rounded dome shapes of various sizes;

2 shrubs that can be developed into taller, more complex shapes;

3 plants with more open, feathery outlines;

4 bamboos and grasses, for their foliage effects;

5 trees, for their high-level foliage and their trunks.

Dome-shaped plants

To create rounded shapes, plants with small, fine leaves are ideal. Such plants will also need to tolerate regular pruning, or have a naturally neat habit. Suitable plants include Japanese holly (*Ilex crenata*) and box (*Buxus sempervirens*). Hebes are a large family that has a number of useful plants, such as *Hebe buxifolia*. The range of hybrid Japanese evergreen azaleas, which are classified in the genus *Rhododendron*, is very extensive, and a whole gamut of leaf colour, size and flower colour is

Left To create large domes of azaleas, plant different coloured flowering varieties together.

available. Some of the dwarf rhododendrons such as *Rhododendron williamsianum* are also useful, as they are naturally mound-forming plants, as is *R. yakushimanum*, which also has many hybrids, and *Skimmia japonica*.

Shrubs for shaping into specimens

Osmanthus x *burkwoodii* responds to training and pruning and can be grown on to a useful specimen size, 1.5–2.5m (5–8ft). Privet (*Ligustrum ovalifolium*) is also very easy to shape into a number of configurations. *Pittosporum tenuifolium*, *Enkianthus campanulatus*, *Berberis thunbergii*, and *Corokia cotoneaster* can all be pruned into interesting shapes. Hedging plants can also be shaped – *Cotoneaster simonsii*,

hornbeam (*Carpinus betulus*), beech (*Fagus sylvatica*), *Euonymus obovatus*, *Pyracantha rogersiana* and yew (*Taxus baccata*) all abide pruning and shaping.

Feathery plants

Plants with an open, feathery texture are useful for creating softer outlines and foliage gradients in the background of a composition, and also to act as a foil to plants with tighter outlines. These include *Spiraea albiflora*, *Deutzia gracilis* and *Fothergilla major* (which also has fiery autumn colours).

Bamboos and grasses

There are many bamboos that can be used as specimens as well as for background planting effects. *Phyllostachys bissetii*, *P. aureosulcata* 'Spectabilis', *P.*

nigra and *Arundinaria anceps* all make good specimen plants. Bamboos work particularly well set in the background of a water basin feature (see pages 64–5), especially when the vertical lines created by the bamboo are underplanted with *Hosta sieboldiana* for a striking, sculptural combination. Of the grasses, *Molinia caerulea* 'Overdam', *Stipa calamagrostis* and *Miscanthus sinensis* are highly effective when planted in drifts. The winter foliage of russet colours works well as a backdrop to stones, as does the movement provided by the slender stems, contrasted with the solidity of the rock.

Trees

In the Japanese garden, the designer seeks a balance in the proportion of the elements of the composition. Trees can present a problem in so much as they can, if not controlled, upset that balance over a period of time by growing too large for the space available. Therefore, you should give serious consideration to the choice of trees. Pines such as *Pinus thunbergii*, *P. parviflora* and *P. densiflora* are probably the most used trees in the gardens in Japan. There are many specimens of great age surviving, principally due to the consistent pruning they have received. Pruning and developing pine trees for your own garden is certainly a challenge, but not impossible. *Pinus sylvestris*, the Scots pine, and the dwarf pines *P. sylvestris* 'Watereri' and *P. mugo*, can be used successfully for this purpose. White-stemmed birches such as *Betula jacquemontii* can add a strong accent, though they will grow well and will require space. Trees such as *Styrax obassia*, *Stewartia pseudocamellia* and *Cornus controversa* are relatively slow-growing and can be pruned. Conifers, such as *Cedrus deodara*, are fast to establish, and will respond to pruning and training; though they will require regular attention, as they can produce plenty of juvenile foliage.

Right The soft lines of grasses will last long into the winter months.

Plants commonly used in Japanese gardens

Hardiness zones

Hardiness zones are defined by the lowest winter temperature obtained in a particular area. There are 11 zones, with Zone 1 being the coldest. A plant will normally survive in the zone or zones indicated and in other, warmer zones, although some plants will not survive in climates that are too hot.

Zone 1	below -46°C (-50°F)
Zone 2	-46 – -40°C (-50 – -40°F)
Zone 3	-40 – -34°C (-40 – -30°F)
Zone 4	-34 – -29°C (-30 – -20°F)
Zone 5	-29 – -23°C (-20 – -10°F)
Zone 6	-23 – -18°C (-10 – 0°F)
Zone 7	-18 – -12°C (0 – 10°F)
Zone 8	-12 – -7°C (10 – 20°F)
Zone 9	-7 – -1°C (20 – 30°F)
Zone 10	-1 – 4°C (30 – 40°F)
Zone 11	above 4°C (above 40°F)

Acer palmatum
Japanese maple
Momiji maple

A spreading, rounded, deciduous tree, grown for its attractive leaves and autumn colouration. There are hundreds of cultivars, offering a wide range of leaf form and colour.

- **Cultivation** Plant in sun or semi-shade, with protection from cold, drying winds.
- **Soil** Grow in well-drained, moisture-retentive, fertile soil.
- **Height x spread** 8 x 10m (25 x 30ft)
- **Hardiness** Zones 5–8

Berberis thunbergii
Barberry
Megi

A compact, deciduous shrub, this has light green leaves which turn vivid red and orange in autumn. Pale yellowish flowers are followed by small red berries.

- **Cultivation** Grow in sun or semi-shade.
- **Soil** Berberis are tolerant of a wide range of soil types as long as they are well drained.
- **Height x spread** 1.8 x 2.4m (6 x 8ft)
- **Hardiness** Zone 4

Camellia japonica
Camellia
Tsubaki

An evergreen shrub, with glossy, dark green leaves and flowers in white, pink or red in early spring. There are numerous cultivars, with different flower types and colours and habits of growth.

- **Cultivation** Protect plants from cold, drying winds and from direct early-morning sun.
- **Soil** Camellias must have rich, moisture-retentive, well-drained, acid soil.
- **Height x spread** 3–9 x 4–8m (10–28 x 12–25ft)
- **Hardiness** Zones 7–8

Chamaecyparis obtusa (syn. *Cupressus obtusa*)
Hinoki cypress
Hinoki

A conical, fairly fast-growing, evergreen coniferous tree, with dark green leaves, marked with white on the undersides. The cones are round and scaly.

- **Cultivation** Grow in full sun and trim back lightly (if necessary) in spring or autumn.
- **Soil** Plant in neutral to acid, moisture-retentive but well-drained soil.
- **Height x spread** 20 x 6m (70 x 20ft)
- **Hardiness** Zone 6

Cornus kousa
Dogwood, kousa
Yamaboshi

A deciduous shrub or small tree. The dark green leaves turn orange-red or purple in autumn, and in summer greenish flowers are surrounded by white bracts.

- **Cultivation** Grow in sun or semi-shade and protect from spring frosts.
- **Soil** Plant in neutral to acid, moisture-retentive but well-drained soil.
- **Height x spread** 7 x 5m (22 x 15ft)
- **Hardiness** Zone 5

Cryptomeria japonica
Japanese cedar
Sugi

An evergreen coniferous tree with bright green or grey-green leaves, which may turn bronze in winter. There are several attractive cultivars, including some dwarf forms.

- **Cultivation** Protect young trees from cold, drying winds and plant in sun or semi-shade.
- **Soil** Cryptomerias need rich, deep, acid, moisture-retentive but free-draining soil.
- **Height x spread** 25 x 6m (80 x 20ft)
- **Hardiness** Zone 6

Daphne odora
Winter daphne
Jinchoge

An excellent, rounded, evergreen shrub, bearing very fragrant purple-pink and white flowers from midwinter to early spring. The leaves are dark, glossy green, and the flowers are followed by red fruit.

- **Cultivation** Grow in sun or semi-shade in a sheltered spot. Established plants should not be moved.
- **Soil** Plant in well-drained, rich soil and mulch well to keep the roots cool.
- **Height x spread** 1.5 x 1.5m (5 x 5ft)
- **Hardiness** Zone 7

Enkianthus campanulatus
Sarasa dodan

A tree-like, spreading shrub, this has mid-green leaves, which turn vivid orange, yellow and red in autumn. Little, cream-yellow flowers are borne in racemes in late spring to early summer.

- **Cultivation** Grow in full sun or semi-shade in a site sheltered from cold, drying winds.
- **Soil** Plant in well-drained but moisture-retentive, neutral to acid soil that has been enriched with leaf mould.
- **Height x spread** 5 x 4m (15 x 12ft)
- **Hardiness** Zone 5

Fatsia japonica (syn. Aralia japonicum A. sieboldii)
Japanese aralia, Japanese fatsia
Yatsude

The glossy, dark green leaves of this suckering, evergreen shrub are deeply lobed. In autumn sprays of white-cream flowers are borne above the foliage.

- **Cultivation** Grow in a sheltered position in full sun or light shade. It must be protected from cold, drying winds.
- **Soil** Plant in moist but well-drained, rich soil.
- **Height x spread** 4 x 4m (12 x 12ft)
- **Hardiness** Zone 8

Ginkgo biloba
Maidenhair tree
Icho

An elegant, coniferous, deciduous tree with exceptionally attractive, fan-shaped leaves, which turn golden-yellow in autumn. These trees are tolerant of atmospheric pollution.

- **Cultivation** Grow in full sun or light shade.
- **Soil** Plant in any rich, well-drained soil.
- **Height x spread** 30 x 8m (100 x 25ft)
- **Hardiness** Zone 4

Hemerocallis fulva
Daylily
Yabu kanzo

The trumpet-shaped flowers of this clump-forming, rhizomatous perennial are rusty orange. They are borne in mid- to late summer on erect stems above the bluish-green leaves.

- **Cultivation** Grow in full sun.
- **Soil** Daylilies need rich, moisture-retentive but well-drained soil.
- **Height x spread** 1 x 1.2m (3 x 4ft)
- **Hardiness** Zone 4

Iris ensata (syn. I kaempferi)
Japanese water iris
Hana shobu

In early to midsummer this beardless Laevigate iris has variably purple flowers with a yellow streak on the falls. Three or four flowers are borne on each stem.

- **Cultivation** Grow in full sun.
- **Soil** These irises will not tolerate lime and must have reliably moist, humus-rich soil.
- **Height x spread** 1 x 0.15m (3ft x 6in)
- **Hardiness** Zones 5–9

Kerria japonica
Jew's mantle, Japanese rose
Yamabuki

This deciduous, suckering shrub bears masses of bright yellow flowers on arching stems in mid- to late spring. The leaves are bright green.

- **Cultivation** Grow in sun or semi-shade.
- **Soil** Kerrias will grown in any rich, well-drained soil.
- **Height x spread** 2 x 2.5m (6 x 8ft)
- **Hardiness** Zone 4

Magnolia stellata
Star magnolia
Shide kobushi

A slow-growing, eventually rather spreading shrub, this bears exquisite, sometimes pink-flushed, white flowers in early spring, before the leaves appear.

- **Cultivation** Grow in sun or partial shade in a position sheltered from cold, drying winds. Apply a mulch of leaf mould in early spring.
- **Soil** This species will grow in almost any rich, well-drained but moisture-retentive soil, although it will not do well on chalk.
- **Height x spread** 3 x 4m (10 x 12ft)
- **Hardiness** Zone 4

Mahonia japonica
Oregon grape, holly grape
Hiragi nanten

This upright shrub has glossy green, evergreen leaves and large racemes of fragrant, bright yellow flowers in winter to early spring. The flowers are followed by purplish berries.

- **Cultivation** Grow in shade or semi-shade.
- **Soil** Mahonias need rich, moisture-retentive but well drained soil.
- **Height x spread** 2 x 3m (6 x 10ft)
- **Hardiness** Zone 6

Miscanthus sinensis
Eulalia, Japanese silver grass
Susuki

A deciduous grass with blue-green leaves and pale grey, purple-tinged spikelets of flowers in autumn.

- **Cultivation** Grow in full sun and protect from winter wet.
- **Soil** This needs fairly rich, moisture-retentive but well-drained soil.
- **Height x spread** 3 x 1.2m (10 x 4ft)
- **Hardiness** Zones 4–6

Nandina domestica
Heavenly bamboo
Nanten

An evergreen, sometimes semi-evergreen, shrub with upright shoots and bright green leaves. When they are young and in autumn the leaves are reddish-purple.

- **Cultivation** Plant in a sunny, sheltered site.
- **Soil** Grow in rich, well-drained soil.
- **Height x spread** 2 x 1.5m (6 x 5ft)
- **Hardiness** Zone 7

Osmanthus fragrans
Sweet tea, fragrant olive
Gin mokusei

A small tree or upright, evergreen shrub, this has glossy, dark green leaves. In autumn, also sometimes in spring, fragrant, white flowers are borne in clusters; they are followed by bluish fruit.

- **Cultivation** Grow in sun or semi-shade and protect from cold, drying winds.
- **Soil** Osmanthus need rich, well-drained soil.
- **Height x spread** 6 x 6m (20 x 20ft)
- **Hardiness** Zone 9

Paeonia suffruticosa
Moutan, tree peony
Botan

An upright, deciduous bush with dark green leaves. White, pink, red or purple flowers are borne in late spring or early summer.

- **Cultivation** Grow in full sun or semi-shade and protect from cold, drying winds.

- **Soil** Peonies need deep, humus-rich, moist but well-drained soil.
- **Height x spread** 2.1 x 2.1m (7 x 7ft)
- **Hardiness** Zone 7

Photinia glabra
Japanese photinia
Kaname mochi

A rounded, evergreen shrub, this has dark green leaves that are red when they first emerge. In summer small white flowers are borne in clusters and are followed by red-black berries.

- **Cultivation** Grow in sun and protect from cold, drying winds.
- **Soil** This species needs rich, moist but well-drained soil.
- **Height x spread** 3 x 3m (10 x 10ft)
- **Hardiness** Zone 7

Phyllostachys bambusoides
Giant timber bamboo
Ma-dake

This is a clump-forming bamboo, bearing large, glossy green leaves on thick, deep green canes.

- **Cultivation** Grow in full sun.
- **Soil** Plant in rich, moisture-retentive but well-drained soil.
- **Height x spread** 8m (25ft) x indefinite
- **Hardiness** Zone 7

Phyllostachys nigra
Black bamboo
Kuro chiku

A clump-forming bamboo, this has dark green leaves borne on arching, black canes.

- **Cultivation** Grow in full sun.
- **Soil** Plant in rich, moisture-retentive but well-drained soil.
- **Height x spread** 5 x 3m (15 x 10ft)
- **Hardiness** Zone 7

Pinus parviflora
Japanese white pine
Goyo matsu

This evergreen conifer has dark green leaves, with blue on the inner sides. The oblong cones are reddish-brown.

- **Cultivation** Grow in full sun.
- **Soil** Grow in deep, rich, well-drained soil; this species will not do well on chalk.
- **Height x spread** 20 x 8m (70 x 25ft)
- **Hardiness** Zone 5

Pinus thunbergii
Japanese black pine
Kuro matsu

A rounded, evergreen conifer with grey-green leaves and grey-purple bark. The oblong cones are greenish-brown.

- **Cultivation** Grow in full sun.
- **Soil** Grow in deep, rich, well-drained soil.
- **Height x spread** 25 x 8m (80 x 25ft)
- **Hardiness** Zone 6

Prunus serrulata (syn. P. jamasakura)
Hill cherry, Japanese mountain cherry
Yama zakura

A deciduous tree with a spreading habit. The leaves, bronze-red when they emerge, turn dark green and then red and yellow in autumn. White flowers, borne in mid- to late spring, are followed by red fruit.

- **Cultivation** Grow in full sun.
- **Soil** Plant in moist, rich, well-drained soil.
- **Height x spread** 12 x 12m (40 x 40ft)
- **Hardiness** Zone 5

Pseudosasa japonica (syn. Arundinaria japonica)
Arrow bamboo, metake
Ya dake

This spreading, rhizomatous bamboo has dark green leaves and dark green canes that age to light brown.

- **Cultivation** Grow in full sun or semi-shade. Cut back plants that flower to ground level.
- **Soil** Grow in moist, rich soil.
- **Height x spread** 6m (20ft) x indefinite
- **Hardiness** Zone 6

Rhododendron indicum
Rhododendron
Satsuki

A low-growing, rather spreading evergreen shrub with variable, funnel-shaped, bright red or pink flowers in late spring.

- **Cultivation** Plant in semi-shade.
- **Soil** Grow in moist, humus-rich, well-drained acid soil.
- **Height x spread** 2 x 2m (6 x 6ft)
- **Hardiness** Zone 6

Rhododendron mollis
Azalea
Renge tsutsuji

A small deciduous shrub with funnel-shaped, yellow or orange flowers in spring.

- **Cultivation** Plant in semi-shade.
- **Soil** Grow in moist, humus-rich, well-drained acid soil.
- **Height x spread** 1.2 x 1.2m (4 x 4ft)
- **Hardiness** Zone 7

Spiraea thunbergii
Spiraea, bridal wreath
Yuki yanagi

A deciduous or semi-evergreen shrub, with arching branches. Clusters of white flowerheads are borne in early spring.

- **Cultivation** Grow in full sun and prune after flowering if needed.
- **Soil** Spiraeas need rich, moisture-retentive but well-drained soil.
- **Height x spread** 1.5 x 1.8m (5 x 6ft)
- **Hardiness** Zone 4

Wisteria floribunda
Japanese wisteria
Fuji

A vigorous deciduous climber, grown for its wonderful racemes of fragrant, violet-blue flowers. The leaves are mid-green.

- **Cultivation** Grow in full sun; unless allowed to grow into and over a tree, they need training and regular pruning.
- **Soil** Plant in rich, moisture-retentive but well-drained soil.
- **Height** 9m (28ft)
- **Hardiness** Zone 5

PRUNING AND TRAINING

Gardens are organic and living things, and are therefore in a constant state of change – from one season to the next, from one moment to the next. Management of plants is a key element in the success of a garden in the long term. Whenever one is in close contact with plants that have been alive for many years, there is a particular sense of wonder.

In some gardens in Japan, there are trees that are hundreds of years old, which have been tended by successive generations of gardeners. Part of the reason for their longevity is that the plants have received regular and correct pruning and training. Pruning in the Japanese garden is carried out for three main reasons:

1 to shape the plant, with the aim of maintaining an overall balance and proportion of all elements within the garden space;

2 to reveal the shape of the trunk, in the case of trees and large shrub specimens; the foliage is then gathered into clusters of 'cloud' shapes, usually in an asymmetrical pattern;

3 to maintain the health and vigour of the plant, by encouraging renewal through the production of new growing shoots.

Pruning for shape

Shaping of plants, particularly shrubs and trees, can start at an early age. Indeed there are many advantages to starting early. The plant is easier to develop into a prescribed pattern, the rate of growth will be at its most vigorous, and the basic material will not cost too much to purchase initially. Plants can be grown on in large containers, which will allow for plenty of root growth, and then planted out at a later date when the shape is more developed; alternatively, shrubs and trees

Left A well-developed plant can act as a significant focal point in the garden. One tree can evoke an entire landscape.

Opposite The layered framework of branches can be achieved by tying branches to canes, then trimming all the foliage below the canes.

can be planted in their final position, and worked on there. Growing and developing your own stock of plants has many satisfactions – not least seeing your handiwork change and mature over the years. Today it is also possible to obtain quite large nursery stock, which gives the benefit of being able to work with reasonably mature material in pots.

For plants such as azaleas and other low ground-cover shrubs, simply clip with shears into tight, mounded forms. Where they are planted in association with rockery stones, they can appear to hug and support the stones.

Larger, domed shapes can also be achieved with plants such as holly (*Ilex* spp.) and tall-growing shrubs such as *Photinia* 'Red Robin', *Pittosporum tenuifolium* and *Olearia* x *haastii*. They will require pruning at regular intervals with shears to maintain their shape and proportion.

Also look at what is already available in the garden and decide whether it is suitable for pruning. This can be a fast-track method of producing large, shaped plants. There are limitations, though; the plant may not be in the most suitable place for the scheme, and moving a large, established plant is fraught with risk. It can be done, with meticulous preparation and patience, though there will always be a chance that the move may not be successful. Plants that form dense mats of root, such as rhododendrons and bamboos, are generally easier to move than plants that can send out far-reaching roots, such as pines and most other trees. If you have large, established plants, it is probably better to see if they can be used where they are, rather than risk the upheaval caused by moving them.

Pruning trees and large shrubs

Generally, the pruning of larger specimens is a matter of looking closely at the plant to assess what the basic structure of the plant is like. Is the stem straight, or is it leaning to one side? Where do most of the bigger, thicker branches lie? Is the distribution of the main branches dispersed fairly equally over the plant, or are they more to one side? The plant will require careful examination to determine the possibilities contained within the existing structure. The pruning is designed to reveal a shape that will already be defined within the plant.

Begin by removing all the weak secondary growth (branches that do not form part of the main framework of the plant), working towards the main trunk. Make each cut as neat as possible, ensuring you do not leave any stubs of branches behind. Then, having decided which of the principal branches are worth saving, cut away the rest one by one. After each cut, look to see the effect that the removal has on the shape that is emerging. The general pattern you are looking for has larger 'pads' of foliage extending on branches emanating from the main stem near the base, and shorter, tighter pads towards the top. Always look to maintain a balanced distribution of branch pads. Thinning or opening the crown will allow light and air to penetrate right through the plant structure. This also has the benefit that the lower branches will remain healthy, and not die because the spreading crown above is blocking their light.

The complete look you are trying to achieve is that of the shape of an old plant. Look in fields and parks at old trees. Observe them from a distance, and see how the branches are gathered together to make the characteristic shape of the mature tree. It is this that you are trying to reproduce in the younger plant you are shaping. Tree trunks will quite often describe an 'S' shape; this is considered to be both balanced and dynamic. An important consideration is to observe and maintain a horizontal line at the base of the pad, while the top of the pad can take on a billowing or rounded shape. Avoid arranging foliage pads directly over one another. Overall, the tree or shrub should be shaped to fit within the outline of an asymmetrical triangle.

PRUNING SHAPES

clipped, rounded shape

multi-stem with pads arranged at various heights

tall, straight stem with pads

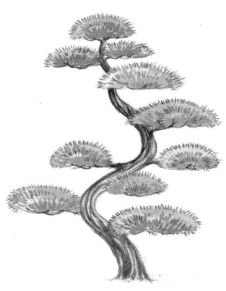

S-shaped trunk

Left The shape and texture of planting in a Japanese garden is more important than colour.

Sometimes the lower branches are deliberately extended, and as you progress up the plant the length of the pads shortens in distance from the main stem. This arrangement also allows light and air to reach all the pads of foliage.

Routine pruning

To maintain health and vigour in your trees and shrubs, you should regularly prune out branches that cross, branches that are growing back towards the main stem, and branches growing directly upwards or downwards from the main stem. Some plants, such as grasses, only require selective thinning from time to time. Trim any dome-shaped shrubs regularly to maintain their form. The key with all pruning is to study and observe the natural tendency of the plant, allow the plant to grow in the way it naturally responds to its environment, and select and manipulate the shape from that point. Thus you will be working with the plant, and not forcing it.

Training

You can train plants from an early stage by bending the stems into the desired position and holding them in place with canes pushed into the ground. Usually a season or two is enough to develop a pronounced shape. You can also tie weights to the ends of branches to achieve a flattening of the branches. It is important that any ties are checked frequently, or they will cut into the growing bark and produce a scar. Ties may need adjusting twice a year, at which time you should loosen and retie them. Usually two growing seasons are sufficient to set the pattern for most branches. A conifer such as *Cedrus atlantica* has branches with a natural tendency to grow upwards, and may need longer.

GARDEN MAINTENANCE

Creating any manner of garden has implications for the future – the garden will need looking after. There is no such beast as the 'no-maintenance garden'; even a concrete yard needs sweeping. The Japanese-style garden is as difficult or as easy as you make it, so you should seriously consider future maintenance requirements at the planning stage (see pages 12–15).

Where you are using gravel areas, for example, always place a layer of geotextile sheeting underneath (see page 30), and lay the gravel to a depth of at least 8cm (3in). You will need to consider how the gravel is to be contained within its prescribed area (see page 31). Always use treated timber for decking areas or fence posts, as this will last longer. When planning a bog garden, remember that weeds will grow quite happily in a damp environment, and that you will require some form of access through the area.

Like any garden space, the more you cherish and enjoy it the greater the rewards you will reap. Japanese gardens can certainly be created to be

Right Keeping the garden tidy allows the eye to linger over the details of a composition. A change of light can cause different aspects of the garden to come into play.

Left Larger water features will need to be given attention throughout the year to keep them clear of algae, and falling leaves in autumn.

low maintenance in terms of the number of hours required per year to keep the garden looking good. The gardens score highly on visual impact and style, and maintenance of the garden is important if you are to continue to satisfy the eye of the viewer. The pleasure in maintaining a garden is coming to understand every part of it, knowing each plant, its individual habits, likes and dislikes, and observing the small but significant changes that constantly take place. The garden is a creative laboratory, where you can try out your ideas; inevitably, some will work better than others. Maintaining the garden provides you with an opportunity to learn, by observing and following the lead of what is happening. By influencing what is happening, the gardener can put his or her own mark on the garden. It is, after all, a partnership. Above all, work with nature, get to know your garden well,

Right Bamboo is revered in Japan for its temporary nature. It is not expected to last for ever and will need replacing fairly regularly.

and the enjoyment and pleasure that comes flowing back to you will be multiplied many times. Then the garden truly can be a place of peace and tranquillity.

There are two main threads to maintaining a Japanese garden in tip-top shape: routine tasks to keep the garden looking clean and tidy, and caring for the plants. Tidiness in the presentation of the garden is a major part of the aesthetic of the garden culture in Japan. It is particularly true of the Tea Garden, where cleanliness is sacrosanct. There is an illustrative story concerning maintenance and Tea Gardens. The Tea Master Sen no Rikyu and his son were preparing for a ceremony during the season of cherry blossom. The garden was immaculately swept, and every flower petal was cleared

from the ground. The place was pristine, and all the stone paths were sprinkled with water to freshen them. As Rikyu inspected the garden, he reached up and gently shook a bough of the blossom tree, scattering petals across the garden. 'Now it is perfect,' he declared.

Routine tasks

1 Clear away all fallen leaves. For keeping gravel areas tidy, the kind of garden vacuum cleaner available today that can suck up leaves as well as blow them is a boon. Try to clear the leaves when they are dry, because it is much easier than when they are wet.

2 Remove all weeds as soon as you see them.

3 Compost any fallen leaves, weeds and shredded plant prunings, and put the resulting well-rotted compost back onto the garden.

4 Where you have areas of bare soil around plants, apply a layer of mulch to help retain moisture during dry periods by cutting down evaporation from the surface. Mulches include composted bark, crushed slate and gravel. The texture and colours of bark mulch also provide another design opportunity.

5 Re-treat timber regularly with preservative to prolong its life, and replace any bamboo canes that have rotted.

Installing drainage

ground level

backfilled soil

crushed stones
and gravel

perforated
pipe

If you discover that parts of the garden are very damp or even prone to flooding, then you should consider installing drainage in the relevant area. This should ideally be done at an early stage in the garden construction, but can be added later if it proves to be necessary. Changing a garden's contours will affect the surface run-off, and this can lead to water appearing where it did not settle previously. If you are considering making alterations to the ground

shape, then think about what effect this will have on the drainage system in the garden.

To make a simple 'soakaway' drain, dig a hole about 90cm (3ft) wide and at least 2m (7ft) deep, at the lowest point in the area. Place a layer of crushed stones and gravel in the bottom of the hole, 1.2m (4ft) deep, and fill the rest of it with topsoil. If this is not sufficient to allow excess water to drain away, you will need to dig a trench and lay a perforated plastic

pipe in the bottom of it, surrounded by a layer of large-diameter gravel or crushed stones. If you then lead the pipe to the nearest drain, or to a deeper drainage ditch, you will manage to drain the affected area as required.

Using a system of connected drains, laid in the same way as above, running from the top of a slope to the bottom, water can be directed into a low-lying damp area to create a bog garden (see page 39).

Caring for plants

You should inspect and observe plants in the garden on a regular basis. Keep an eye on any form of binding around branches, where plants are being trained, as this needs loosening from time to time (see page 151).

Established plants planted in open ground will need watering during long, dry spells. The soil in containers tends to dry out fast so containers will need regular watering – up to twice a day in summer. Yellowed leaves or wilting will indicate that your plants need water.

All plants need to be kept supplied with nutrients to thrive. Apply a slow-release fertilizer to established plants in open ground in early summer. A thick layer of bulky organic material – such as manure, cocoa shells or bark – will slowly decompose and enrich the soil.

Left The large, distinctively shaped flowers of *Magnolia stellata* give the tree its common name – star magnolia.

INDEX

Index

ACKNOWLEDGEMENTS

Executive Editor: Emily van Eesteren
Editor: Sharon Ashman
Copy-editor: Alison Copland
Senior Designer: Peter Burt
Designer: Mark Stevens
Illustrator: Gill Tomblin
Picture Research: Christine Junemann
Production Controller: Viv Cracknell
Index: Hilary Bird

Corbis UK Ltd/Kevin R. Morris 120, /Joel W. Rogers 53, /Michael S. Yamashita 4, 7, 25 left, 30, 36, 41, 49, 78, 93, 97, 112, 127, 129

Garden Picture Library/David Askham 101, /Peter Baistow 26, /Brian Carter 125, /Eric Crichton 2, 103, /Michael Diggin 138, 140, /John Ferro Sims 155, /Juliet Greene 123, /John Glover 12 /Des. Hiroshi Nannori, RHS Chelsea Flower Show 1996 19, /Juliet Greene, 'A Taste of Japan Garden', RHS Hampton Court Flower Show 1999 28, /Roger Hyam 98, /Michael Paul 1, 40, 42, /Jerry Pavia 37 left, 106, 141 top, /JS Sira 13, 14, /Ron Sutherland 32, 35, 39, 44, 46, 77, 81, 82, 108, 115, 152, /Brigitte Thomas 37 right, /Steven Wooster 47, 85

Jerry Harpur 141 bottom, 142, 148, /Kyoto Temple Garden 6, 8, 10, 43, 48, 87, /Japanese Stroll Garden NY 18 right, 153, /Japanese Garden, Portland, Oregon 16, 23, 29, 75, /Blocdel Reserve, Bainbridge Island, USA 27, /Hakone Garden, Saratoga, CA 69, /Design; Terry Welch 107, /Design; Mrs Pomeroy CA 149

Nigel Hicks 25 right, 45, 111, 151

Andrea Jones/Garden Exposures 34

Robert Ketchell 17, 31, 38, 94, 105, 117, 135, 143, 144

Andrew Lawson 52 right, 83, /Des. John van Hage, RHS Chelsea Flower Show 1996 136, /Jojakko-Ji, Kyoto, Japan 132, /RHS Garden, Wisley 52 left, /Feng Shui Garden, Des. Pamela Woods, RHS Hampton Court Flower Show 1999 154,

Clive Nichols Photography/COA garden, Des. Hiroshi Nanamori, RHS Chelsea Flower Show 1996 73, /Des. Natural & Oriental Water Gardens/Garden & Security Lighting, RHS Hampton Court Flower Show 1997 55, 56, /Des. R. Ketchell/E. Tunnell, RHS Hampton Court Flower Show 1996 59, 67, /Des. Spidergarden.com, Lighting by Cotsworld Electrical, RHS Chelsea Flower Show 2000 54, /Honda Tea Garden, des. J. Dowle & K. Ninomiya, RHS Chelsea Flower Show 1995 22

Harry Smith Collection 20, 50, 51, 63, 90, 119, /Primrose Hill Nursery, RHS Chelsea Flower Show 1988 18 left

V & A Picture Library 9